THE HOMERIC EPICS

THE HOMERIC EPICS

C. A. Trypanis

ARIS & PHILLIPS Ltd.,
Warminster, Wiltshire, England

ISBN   cloth   0 85668 085 0
ISBN   paper   0 85668 086 9

Published by Aris & Phillips Ltd., Teddington House,
        Warminster, Wilts., England.

Printed in England by Biddles Ltd., Guildford, Surrey.
Distributed in the USA and Canada by ISBS, PO box 555, Forest Grove, Oregon 97116,
    USA.

CONTENTS

Bibliography   vi

Preface   xi

Chapter One   —   The Poet Homer and the Homeric
                   Question   1

Chapter Two   —   The Structure of the Iliad and the
                   Odyssey   7

Chapter Three —   The date of the Homeric Epics
                   and their form   41

Chapter Four   —   Epic Narrative Technique   59

Chapter Five   —   Men and gods in the Homeric epics   79

Chapter Six   —   The Poetic Achievement of the Homeric
                   epics   98

Chapter Seven —   The Influence of the Homeric epics   103

Index   109

v

BIBLIOGRAPHY

Allen, T. W.   1924 Homer, The Origins and the Transmission. Oxford.
————   1961 Homeri Opera V. Oxford.
Ameis, K. F. - Hentze, C. - Cauer, P.   1964 Homerus, Odyssee. Amsterdam.
————   1965 Ilias. Amsterdam.
d'Aubignac, F. H.   1604-76 Conjectures Académiques; ou Dissertation sur l'Iliade.
                           Paris.
Bassett, S. F.   1938 The Poetry of Homer. Berkeley.
Bechtel, F.   1901 Die Sprachform der Urilias. Robert, C. 258-265.
————   1908 Die Vocalcontraction bei Homer. Halle.
Bethe, E.   1914 Homer, Dichtung und Saga I. Leipzig-Berlin.
————   1929² ———————————— II
————   1927 ———————————— III
————   1946 Buch und Bild in Altertum. Leipzig.
Bergk, T.   1872 Griech. Literaturgeschichte I. Berlin
————   1914-18 Poetae Lyrici Greci. Berlin.
Blass, F.   1887-88 Die attische Beredsamkeit I-III. Leipzig.
Bolling, G. M.   1944 The Athetized Lines of the Iliad. Baltimore.
Bowra, C. M.   1930 Tradition and Design in the Iliad. Oxford.
————   1955 Homer and his Forerunners. Edinburgh.
————   1962 Composition. Wace and Stubbings, 19-74.
Bucholz, E.   1871-85 Die homerische Realien I-III. Leipzig.
Bury, J. B.   1951 History of Greece. London.
Busolt, G.   1920 Griech. Staatskunde I (Handb. d. Altertumswiss. IV, I, 1). München.
Carpenter, Rhys   1946 Folktale, Fiction and Saga in the Homeric Epics. Berkeley.
Caskey, J. L.   1966 Excavations in Keos 1964-1965. Hesperia 35, 363-375.
Cauer, P.   1921-1923³ Grundfragen der Homerkritik I-II. Leipzig.
Chadwick, H. M. & N. K. 1932-40 The Growth of Literature I-III. Cambridge.
———— J.   1956 The Greek Dialects and Greek Prehistory. Greece and Rome NS 3,
                           38-50
————   1963 The Prehistory of the Greek Language. CAH² Vol. II, Chap. 39,
                           fasc. 15.
Chantraine, P.   1953 Grammaire homérique II. Paris
————   1953 Les éléments dialectaux de la langue épique. Paris.
————   1942/1958³ Grammaire homérique I. Paris.
Cook, J. M.   1953 Mycenae 1939-1952. BSA 48, 30-68
Croiset, M.   1875 De publicae eloquentiae principiis apud Graecos in homericis
                           carminibus. Paris.

Davison, J. A. 1962 Homeric Criticism. Wace and Stubbings, 215-268.

Delebécque, E.1951 Le Cheval dans l'Iliade. Paris.

Desborough, V. R.d'A. 1967 The Last Myceneans and their Successors. Oxford.

Diehl, E.   1935² Anthologia Lyrica Graeca, fasc. 2. Leipzig.

———   1949³ ——————————   1.

———   1952³ ——————————   3.

Diels, H.   1934⁵ Fragmente der Vorsokratiker I. Berlin.

Dodds, E. R.   1968 Homer. Platnauer, 1-16.

Doerpfeld, W. 1927 Alt-Ithaca. München.

Duckworth, G. E. 1933 Foreshadowing and Suspense in the Epics of Homer,
                    Apollonius and Vergil. Princeton.

Düntzer, H.   1872 Homerische Abhandlungen. Leipzig.

Ebeling, E.   1880-85 Lex. Homericum. Leipzig.

Fenik, B.   1968 Typitcal Battle Scenes in the Iliad. Hermes Einzelschriften 21.

Fick, A.   1883 Die homerische Odyssee. Göttingen.

———   1886 Die homerische Ilias. Göttingen.

Finley, M. J.   1956 The World of Odysseus. London.

———   - Caskey, J. L. - Kirk, G. S. - Page, D. L. 1964 The Trojan War.
                    JHS 84, 1-20

Finsler, G. S. 1912 Homer in der Neuzeit von Dante bis Goethe. Leipzig.

———   1918 - 1924³ Homer I-III. Leipzig.

Focke, F.   1943 Die Odyssee. Stuttgart-Berlin.

Fraccaroli, G. 1903 L'Irrazionale nella letteratura. Torino.

Fränkel, H.   1921 Die homerische Gleichnisse. Göttingen.

Friedländer, P.1948 Epigrammata. Berkeley.

Geffcken, J.   1926 Griech. Lit. Gesch. I. Heidelberg.

Girard, P.   1902 Comment a du se former l'Iliade. Rev. des. ét. Grecques 15,
                    229-287.

Glotz, G.   1904 La solidarité de la famille dans le droit criminel en Grèce. Paris

Gray, D. H. F. 1967 "Homeric epithets for things." Kirk, 55-67.

———   1968 Homer and the Archaeologists. Platnauer, 24-49

Grote, G.   1946-56 History of Greece. London.

Hampe, R.   1936 Frühe griechischen Sagenbilder in Böotien. Athens.

Hampl, F.   1962 Das Ilias ist kein Geschichtsbuch. Serta Philol. Aenipontana
                    37-63 (Innsbruck).

Harrison, E.   1960 Notes on Homeric Psychology. Phoenix 14, 63-80.

Hentze, K.   1904 Monologe in der homerischen Epen. Philologus 63, N. F. XVII,
                    12f.

Hermann, G.   1832 De interpolationibus Homerii. Lipsiae.

Heubeck, A.   1949 Klingner, Über dievier ersten Bücher der Odyssee (rev.).
                    Gnomon 21, 166-167.

———   1954 Der Odyssee - Dichter und die Ilias. Erlangen.

——————— 1957 Hampe, Die homerische Welt im Licht der neuesten Ausgrabun-
gen; Bowra, Homer and his Forerunners (rev.). Gnomon 29,
38-46.

——————— 1961 Page, History and the Homeric Iliad (rev.). Gnomon 33, 113-120.

Jacoby, F. 1933 Die geistige Physiognomie der Odyssee. Die Antike 9, 159-194.

——————— 1944 Patrios Nomos: State Burial in Athens and the Public Cemetery
of the Kerameikos. JHS 64, 37-66.

——————— 1922/1957² Fragmente der griech. Historiker I. 2. Leiden.

Jaeger, W. 1960² Paedeia (trans. G. Highet). New York

Jebb, R. 1887 Homer: An Introduction. Boston.

Jones, J. W. 1956 Law and Legal Theory of the Greeks. Oxford.

Kakrides, J. T. 1949 Homeric Researches. Lund.

Κακριδής, I.Θ 1954 Ὁμηρικά Θέματα. Θεσσαλονίκη.

——————— 1971 Ξαναγυρίζοντας στὸν Ὅμηρο. Θεσσαλονίκη.

Kirchoff, A. 1879² Die homerische Odyssee und ihre Entstellung. Berlin.

Kirk, G. S. 1962 The Songs of Homer. Cambridge.

——————— 1966 Studies in some Technical Aspects of Homeric Style. Formular
Language and Oral Poetry. Yale Class. Studies 20, 73-152. 153-
174.

——————— 1964/1967² The Language and Background of Homer. Cambridge.

Kohl, J. W. 1917 De Chorizontibus (Doctoral Thesis). Giessen.

Κομνηνοῦ - Κακριδῆ, Ο. 1947 Σχέδιο καὶ Τεχνικὴ τῆς Ἰλιάδος. Ἀθήνα.

——————— 1969 ——————————— Ὀδύσσειας. Θεσσαλονίκη.

Lachmann, K. 1837/1841 Betrachtungen über Homers Ilias. Abhandl. d. Akad. d.
Wiss. zu Berlin (new edition by M. Haupt, 1974).

Latte, K. 1931 Beiträge zum griechischen Strafrecht. Hermes 66, 30-48.

Leaf, W. 1902² The Iliad. London.

Lesky, A. 1947 Thalassa. Wien. (reprinted N.Y. & Warminster 1973).

——————— 1952 Die Homerforschung in der Gegenwart. Wien.

——————— 1966 A History of Greek Literature (trans. J. Willis and G. de Heer).
London.

——————— 1967 Homeros. Der Kleine Pauly 2, 1201-1208.

——————— 1968 Homeros. Pauly-Wissowa RE (Realencyclopaedie der klass.
Altertumswiss.) Suppl. XI, 687-846.

Leumann, M. 1950 Homerische Wörter. Basel.

Lipsius, J. H. 1905-12/1966² Das attische Recht. Leipzig.

Lorimer, L. H. 1950 Homer and the Monuments. London.

Mazon, P. 1942/1967³ Introduction à l'Iliade. Paris.

Meister, K. 1921 Die homerische Kunstsprache. Leipzig.

Merkelbach, R. 1969² Untersuchungen zur Odyssee. München.

Meuli, K. 1921 Odyssee und Argonautica. Basel.

Monro, D. B. 1901 Homer's Odyssey. Oxford.

——————— 1957⁴ The Iliad. Oxford.

———— - Allen, T. W. 1912-1846 Homeri Opera I. V. Oxford.

von der Muehll, P. 1952 Kritisches Hypomnema zur Ilias. Basel.

Murray, G. 1937[3] The Rise of the Greek Epic. Oxford.

Nilsson, M. P. 1933 Homer and Mycenae. London.

Nitzsch, G. W. 1862 Beiträge zur Geschichte der epischen Poesie der Griechen. Leipzig.

Page, D. L. 1955 The Homeric Odyssey. Oxford.

———— 1959 History and the Homeric Iliad. Berkeley-Los Angeles.

Palmer, L. R. 1968 Homer and the Philologists. Platnauer, 17-23.

Parry, A. 1966 Have we Homer's Iliad? Yale Class. Studies 20, 175-216.

———— 1971 The Making of Homeric Verse. Oxford.

——— M. 1928 L'épithète traditionelle dans Homère. Paris.

———— 1930 Studies in the Epic Technique of Oral Verse-making. I Homer and Homeric Style. Harvard Stud. in Class. Phil. 41, 73-148.

———— 1932 Studies in the Epic Technique etc. : II The Homeric Language as the Language of Oral Poetry. Harvard Stud. in Class. Phil. 43, 1-50.

———— 1933 The Traditional Metaphor in Homer. Class. Phil. 28, 30-43.

Pfeiffer, R. 1968 History of Classical Scholarship. Oxford.

Platnauer, M. (ed.) 1968 Fifty Years (and 12) of Classical Scholarship. Oxford.

Reichel, W. 1901 Homerische Waffen. Wien.

Reinhardt, K. 1950 Tradition und Geist. Göttingen.

Richards, I. A. 1926[2]/1959 Principles of Literary Criticism. London.

Rohde, E. 1895 Nekyia. Rheinisches Museum 50, 600-635.

Robert, C. 1901 Studien zur Ilias. Berlin.

——— F. 1950 Homère. Paris.

Ruijgh, C. J. 1957 L'élément Achéen dans la langue épique. Assen.

Sanford, W. B. 1958[2] Odyssey. London.

Schadewaldt, W. 1938 Iliasstudien. (Abh. Sächs. Akad. Wissenschaft, Phil. -Hist. K1. 43.5) Leipzig.

———— 1959[3] Von Homers Welt und Werk. Stuttgart.

Schmid, W. - Stählin, O. 1929/1959[2] Geschichte der griech. Literatur I. (Handb. d. Altertumswiss. VII, I, 1) München.

Schulze, W. 1892 Questiones Epicae. Guterslochae.

Schwartz, E. 1924. Die Odyssee. München.

Schwyzer, E. 1939 Griech. Grammatik. München.

Sheppard, J.T. 1922. The Pattern of the Iliad. London.

Shipp, G. P. 1953 Studies in the Language of Homer, London.

Snell, B. 1955[3] Die Entdeckung des Geistes. Hamburg.

Snodgrass, A. 1964 Early Greek Armour and Weapons. Edinburgh.

Trypanis, C.A. 1963 Brothers fighting together in the Iliad. Rhein. Museums 106, 289-297.

Wace, A. J. B. - Stubbings, F. H. (ed) 1962 A Companion to Homer. London.
Wackernagel, J. 1916 Sprachliche Untersuchungen zu Homer. Göttingen.
Wade-Gery, H. T. 1952 The Poet of the Iliad. Cambridge.
Webster, T. B. L. 1958 From Mycenae to Homer. London.
von Wilamowitz-Moellendorff, U. 1906 Über die ionische Wanderung. Sb. Berlin
                               Akad. Wiss., 59-79 (and 1937, Kleine
                               Schriften V 1. Berlin)
————   1920² Das Ilias und Homer. Berlin.
————   1927a Die Heimkehr der Odysseus. Berlin.
————   1927b Das hom. Epos (lecture). Berlin.
Witte, K.   1913 Homeros. Pauly-Wissowa RE VIII², 2213-2247.
Wolf, F. A.   1795 Prolegomena ad Homerum (3rd ed. R. Peppmüller. 1884).
Wolf, H. J.   1946 Traditio 4, 31f.
Wolf-Hartmut, F. 1956 Verwundung und Tod in der Ilias. Göttingen.
Wood, R.   1776 An Essay on the Original Genius and Writings of Homer, Dublin.

Publishers note

*The translation of the quotations from the Iliad and the Odyssey used in this book and
set in condensed type, are from 'The Iliad' translated by E. V. Rieu (1950) and 'The
Odyssey' translated by E. V. Rieu (1946) both published by Penguin Books Ltd.
These translations were approved by the author on grounds of straightforwardness and
accuracy. © E. V. Rieu 1950 and 1946. Reprinted by permission of Penguin Books
Ltd.*

PREFACE

This brief Introduction to the Homeric Epics was written to help the Greek schoolmasters who teach Homer at the Secondary State-run Schools all over Greece. As many of them do not know foreign languages, and foreign books on Homer are not available in the provinces where most of them live and work, its aim was to acquaint them with the major and indeed most involved problems of the Iliad and the Odyssey as scholarship sees them today. It was also hoped that this short Introduction to the greatest epic poetry of the Western world could be of some use to the students of Classics at the Greek Universities and to the general reader, who would like to get some idea of what scholarship maintains today on the person and the verse of Homer.

At the instigation of some of my Oxford friends, I agreed to have this unpretentious account, which mainly draws on the great works of others, translated into English, so that British and American students could also make use of it. I wish to express my warmest thanks to Mr. William Phelps for all the work and care he has put into his English translation of the Greek text.

Athens, 1976   C. A. Trypanis

CHAPTER ONE – THE POET HOMER AND THE HOMERIC QUESTION

Homer the poet.

It was believed in antiquity that the Iliad and Odyssey were the works of Homer, who was considered to be the greatest of poets. Only a small group of Alexandrian grammarians, the chorizontes, raised objections, maintaining that the two epics were not written by the same person (Kohl 1917; Pfeiffer 1968, 230 n. 7. 213).

Antiquity, however, knew nothing certain about Homer's person or life. Even the name, Homer, was strange, and different fictitious etymologies were proposed for it (Schmid - Stählin 1929, 88 n.2. 89). Out of the mass of spurious information that has come down to us, the only element which may be true is that Homer was a Greek from Ionia, associated particularly with Smyrna and Chios.[1]

The association of Homer with Chios and Smyrna goes back at least to Pindar, who informs us that the Homeridae of Chios, an island guild of rhapsodes, were originally members of Homer's clan, but later were just rhapsodes, with no claim to blood descent.[2] Unfortunately we do not know the provenance of the eponymous guildsmen, nor how loose their

---

1. All this spurious information was in circulation for the very reason that nothing certain was known. The commonest version of Homer's life is to be found in the Lives of Homer (Allen 1961, V, 184f), which were compiled from Hellenistic times onwards, but which contain elements from the Classical period. According to the Lives, Homer was born in Smyrna, lived in Chios and died on Ios. His name was originally Melesigenes, from the river Meles, who was his father; and his mother was the nymph Kritheis. He was also said to be descended from Orpheus, and contemporary with - indeed the cousin of - Hesiod, with whom he competed in Euboea. Other cities tried to link their names with Homer's (Schmid - Stählin 1929, 88, and (n. 2), as is clear from the line: "Smyrna, Chios, Colophon, Ithaca, Pylos, Argos, Athens," (Anth. Pal. XVI, 298). Different versions of this line are mentioned.
2. Pindar, *Nem*. II, 1f, and Schol. ad loc.; Strabo XIV, 1. The existence of Homeridae in Chios in the 6th century is attested by the contemporary chronicler Acousilaus of Argos (Jacoby 1957,[2] I, 2). And it is said that the Chian Homerist Cynaethus was the first to recite Homer's poems at Syracuse in 504 BC. On this v. Bergk 1872, 545 and Davison 1962, 219.

links were with the clan chiefs; whether, for example, they were as loose as those between the Asclepiadae doctors and Asclepius, or the Talthybiadae and the herald Talthybius. (Kirk 1962, 272; Davison 1962, 219).

Antiquity, however, did not regard Homer as the author only of the Iliad and Odyssey. Other narrative hexameter poems, like the *Thebais, Cypria,* the *Hymn to Apollo,* and even the inferior *Margarites* and *Batrachomyomachia* were attributed to him, but with less certainty.[3] That need not be surprising, because later and inferior works are often associated with some great name of the past; and for the Greeks Homer was the poet above all others.

Homer, then, remained "a name without a history, though soon enough it acquired a fable" (Page 1955, 137), and that places him in the period before the 7th century, because almost everything we know about the 8th century derives from oral tradition, while from the 7th century onwards, when the Greek alphabet had spread, a whole wave of literary and historical works appears. In any case Callinus'[4] reference to Homer gives us a terminus ante quem, and so do the allusions, imitations and the representations on vases, which, according to all the evidence, presuppose the existence of an Iliad, though not necessarily the Iliad we have today.[5] Beyond this limit, however, it is impossible to determine with accuracy just where Homer should be placed chronologically.[6]

---

3.   For these and other works thought in antiquity to be Homeric, v. Schmid - Stählin 1929, 195f.

4.   Frag. 6 (Bergk 1914—15 = Paus. IX, 9, 5), in which Callinus refers to Homer as the author of the *Thebais.*

5.   Such allusions and imitations are found, for example, in: Semonides of Amorgos, frag. 29 (Diehl 1952[3]), who refers to Iliad VI, 146; Tyrtaeus, frag. 7, 21-28 (Diehl 1949[3], cf XXII, 71-76), frag. 8, 31 (1949[3], cf XVI, 215); Alcman, Parth. 12 (Diehl 1935[2], cf IX, 124) etc.; also Friedländer 1948, 53 (cf XVIII, 567). For the representations v. Gray 1968, 48f. We may add here that it is apparent from Herodotus V, 67, 1 that the Homeric epics were recited at Sicyon before 600 BC.

6.   It should be noted that Herodotus (II, 53, 2) puts Homer in the 9th century, while Theopompus (Frag. 203, Jacoby 1957[2]) puts him in the 7th century. In spite of the fact that the name of Homer was known to Xenophanes (Frag. 9-10, Diels 1934[5]) and Heraclitus (Frags. 42 and 56, Diels 1934[5]), it was not connected with the Iliad and the Odyssey. Thucydides (III 104, 4) attributes to Homer the Homeric *Hymn to Apollo,* in which the author says in line 72 that he is blind. It may be due to this line, together with the fact that in Odyssey 8, 63f Demodocus is depicted as blind, that the tradition arose

The Homeric Question.

Although antiquity almost unanimously attributed the authorship of the Iliad and Odyssey to one poet, Homer, in western Europe this notion was contested from the 17th century. The dispute which broke out between the Unitarian and the Analytical students of the Homeric poems was called the Homeric Question and may be reduced in the final analysis to two main points: first, whether each epic separately is the work of a single poet; and second - if the answer to the first question is affirmative - whether the same poet is the author of both poems.[7]

The real battle began when F. A. Wolf published his well-known *Prolegomena ad Homerum* in 1795, even though the ideas expressed there had been put forward earlier by F. H. d'Aubignac (1625), R. Wood (1776) and J. G. Herder. Wolf believed that writing was unknown to Homer and that without the help of writing no poet could compose works as vast as the Iliad and Odyssey. These works, he maintained, had originally been groups of unconnected poems referring to the same events, and the welding of them together into the form in which they have been handed down to us took place in Athens in the 6th century, when they were written down by order of Peisistratus, so that they could be recited at the festival of the Panathenaia.

The Analytical Homerists, who followed Wolf, put forward various views, some more radical and others more reasonable. The most extreme of these appeared in Lachmann's astonishing *Lieder Theorie* (1837). According to him Homeric poetry was nothing more than a fortuitous collection of songs, some sixteen in number, which had been composed at different periods.

After the extreme theory of the Analysts came the Nucleus theory, first propounded by G. Hermann in 1832, and later developed by G. Grote in his *History of Greece* (vol. II). According to this theory the Iliad was gradually built up from a short original ballad about the wrath of Achilles, around which much epic material, relevant and irrelevant,

---

7.   that Homer was a blind poet. On this subject v. Schmid - Stählin 1929, 60, n.3. For a good account of the Homeric Question up to 1887, v. Jebb 1887; from 1887 to 1922, v. Finsler 1924³; from 1924 to 1952, v. Lesky 1952; and from 1952 to 1968, v. Dodds 1968, 1f.

accumulated, and thus in time it acquired its present length. In one form or another this theory became accepted by a majority of the most eminent German and British scholars of the next two generations.[8]

A. Kirchhoff in 1879 was the first to formulate a similar theory for the Odyssey. The basic, original nucleus of the Odyssey was supposed to have been a shorter ballad about the wanderings of Odysseus, which was gradually expanded and developed. Many important scholars followed in Kirchhoff's footsteps.[9]

However, the theory of the original nucleus was rejected in its turn by Wilamowitz (1920), who suggested that Homer came somewhere in the middle of the Iliad's long period of growth and development. Wilamowitz maintained that during the 8th century Homer welded together and remoulded the works of earlier rhapsodes, and then various later poets enlarged and reshaped his work.

Nevertheless Wilamowitz did not succeed in dealing the Nucleus theory a mortal blow. Many of the more modern students [10] of the Iliad returned to it, and in fact they attained a remarkable degree of unanimity among themselves. There were of course many differences, for example when it came to determining the limits of the original ballad about the wrath of Achilles, or defining the successive stages in its subsequent expansion.[11]

The Unitarians on the other hand tried mainly to elucidate the inconsistencies and contradictions that are apparent in the Homeric epics. The earlier representatives of this school, like Albert Lang or Carl Rothe, were overtaken by the more modern Unitarians; these may be divided into 1) naive Unitarians, who preserve a basic belief in the absolute unity of the Homeric epics and the 'originality' of Homer;[12] and 2) moderates, who admit that the epics contain both pre- and post-Homeric elements,

8.   Among them Th. Bergk, W. Christ, E. Meyer, P. Cauer, C. Robert, E. Bethe, Richard Jebb, Walter Leaf, J. B. Bury and Gilbert Murray.
9.   Among them P. von der Muehll, F. Focke, E. Bethe, R. Merkelbach and D. Page.
10.   Especially P. Mazon, P. Chantraine, E. Bethe and W. Theiler.
11.   Bethe, for example (1914-1927), reduces the ballad to 1.500 lines, while Mazon (1948) considers that fourteen whole books of the Iliad belong to this ballad.
12.   Like L. A. Scott, E. Drerup and J. T. Sheppard.

and who do not despise the analytical approach - each of them, naturally to a different degree.[13] In any case the most fruitful work of the Unitarians in recent years has centered around research into Homer's sources.[14]

In the final analysis it would not be far from the truth to say that the differences between the moderate Analysts and the Unitarians lie principally in their different terminology. What the Analysts call 'nuclei' or 'original', the Unitarians call 'sources'. What the Analysts call 'expansion', the Unitarians call 'interpolation'. And yet, for all the similarities, there still remains between the two schools a basically different approach to the problems, which cannot be overlooked.

The long dispute we have just outlined, if it has not solved the Homeric Question, has nevertheless contributed much to the study and understanding of the Greek epic. An important advance was made in this century during the '30s, when it was demonstrated conclusively that the Iliad and Odyssey are oral compositions. This advance was chiefly, though not exclusively[15] due to the work of a young American scholar, Milman Parry, whose premature death prevented him from completing the research which he had begun so brilliantly (1928, 9f).

The premise from which Milman Parry started was that the function of the special Homeric epic technique, with its constant repetition of the same epithets, frequently recurring stock phrases (formulas) and repeated descriptions of certain scenes, was intended to assist the bard when he was improvising. Parry pointed out, for example, that for each of the thirty-seven principal characters in both epics there is a store of stock, descriptive phrases of exactly the same metrical length, extending from the caesura to the end of the line. He also showed that in each case one, and only one such phrase exists, in accordance with the principle of 'epic economy', as he calls it.[16] Parry concluded that this helped the bard to avoid any breakdown in his recital, because if he came to a stop at the caesura, he had only to choose a suitable phrase from his epic stock in

---

13. Among them T. H. Allen, W. Schadewaldt, L. H. Lorimer, C. M. Bowra and H. T. Wade-Gery.
14. As in the works of W. J. Woodhouse, K. Reinhardt, I. T. Kakrides, H. Pestalozzi, E. Howald and W. Schadewaldt.
15. A. Meillet's contribution should not be underrated. v. Parry 1928, 9f.
16. v. Milman Parry's doctorate (1928) and his two long articles (1930; 1932). They and Parry's other works have now been brought together in Parry 1971.

order to complete the verse and meaning. Parry also adduced a negative proof, by showing that such a system of epithets and other conventional phrases, all matched to the metre, is not found among poets who compose their verse in writing, like Apollonius Rhodius. He further showed that a similar technique grew up in the oral poetry of other peoples as well.[17]

Parry's contribution does not lie in the fact that he considered the Homeric poems to be oral compositions. This view, as we have seen, had already been advanced by Robert Wood in 1767, and then developed, for the original form of the epics, by F. A. Wolf. Parry's contribution was that he proved it, and that it is now no longer possible to deny this affirmation.

---

17. This was also demonstrated, independently of Parry, by H. M. and N. K. Chadwick (1932-40).

CHAPTER TWO – THE STRUCTURE OF THE ILIAD AND THE ODYSSEY

The Structure of the Iliad.

There is no doubt that the Homeric epics have a carefully drafted design and a basic structural unity. We can therefore readily sketch the plot of the Iliad in its general outline:

In the ninth year of the Trojan war[1] Agamemnon, lord of nearly all Greece, clashes with Achilles, the most powerful of his supporters. The dispute begins when Agamemnon is obliged to hand back Chryseis, whom he took as a prize after the capture of the city of Chrysa, to her father, Chryses, a priest of Apollo. The Achaeans hope that, by this restitution, there will be an end to the plague which Apollo sent upon the Greek army to punish them for the disrespect shown by Agamemnon to the priest. Agamemnon, wishing to compensate himself for the loss of Chryseis, takes Briseis, Achilles' prize; he, incensed by the insult, retires from the fight together with his Myrmidons. With the withdrawal of Achilles, the Achaeans are forced onto the defensive. The Trojans storm the ditch the Achaeans had dug and the wall they had built around their camp, and the Trojan leader, Hector, sets fire to one of their ships.

Then Achilles, who has refused all the royal gifts proffered by Agamemnon to make him amends, allows Patroclus, his closest friend, to take part in the battle, with the Myrmidons, in order to save the Achaeans. Patroclus, to whom Achilles has lent his own arms, succeeds in repulsing the Trojans, but is killed by Hector beneath the walls of Troy. In an outburst of rage and grief at the death of his friend, Achilles decides to enter the fight again and avenge Patroclus' death. He forces the panic-stricken Trojans to flee and shut themselves up in the city, and in the subsequent single-combat kills Hector before the eyes of his parents and people. He then maltreats the corpse of his conquered enemy and intends

---

1.   According to the myth, to which the Iliad makes constant reference, the cause of the Trojan war was the abduction by Paris, son of King Priam of Troy, of the beautiful Helen, wife of Agamemnon's brother, Menelaus. Agamemnon called on the Achaean leaders, who owed him allegiance, to make war on Priam and bring back Helen.

to throw it to the dogs and vultures. But Hector's father, king Priam, guided by the gods, comes to the Achaeans' camp and offers a ransom for the body of his son. Achilles, confronted by the terrible grief of the old king, who reminds him of his own old father, relents. Priam takes Hector's body back to Troy, and the Iliad ends with an uneasy truce to allow Hector to be buried.

Around this central theme many episodes are gathered, which help both to develop and at the same time to obscure it,[2] so that when we come to study the text more closely, we find ourselves faced with many difficulties and diverse elements that provoke confusion. For example, we can immediately perceive that the myth does not unfold in a natural manner, does not advance smoothly, but proceeds with many retardations and interruptions,[3] pausing over certain episodes that are excessively expanded, and this is a likely indication that these episodes were originally intended to be recited separately.[4]

At the same time a large part of the material, for all its general epic character, is not directly connected with the plot of the Iliad, and this raises doubts not only over the unity of the structure, but also over whether it is the creation of one man. It is, for example, hard to accept that the same poet who composed the first book of the Iliad, in which the will of Zeus - the basic theme of the whole epic - is clearly formulated, can also be the poet of the following nine books, II to X, which have very little to do with I and are often in direct contradiction to it. We can even detect parallel versions that have been inserted into the Iliad

---

2. All attempts to demonstrate that the symmetry of the Iliad's structure resembles the austere form of a Greek temple pediment or the shape of a Geometric vase (v. J. H. Myers and T. B. L. Webster in Webster 1958, 200, n.1. 200f) should be rejected out of hand (v. Kirk 1962, 261f).
3. It is hard for the contemporary reader to share Aristotle's admiration for the structure of the Iliad (*Poetica* 23, 1459 A 30; cf 26, 1462 B 10).
4. This is also obvious from the manner in which many of the books of the Iliad begin and end, from the prologue to the Odyssey ("This is the tale I pray the divine Muse to unfold to us. Begin it, goddess, at whatever point you will."), and from other points in the Homeric epics (I, 189f; 1, 326. And cf I, 604, where the muses sing one after the other).

side by side, like the Testing (*Diapeira*)[5] in II or the Embassy[6] in IX, and many repetitions[7] and contradictions.[8]

These and many similar difficulties[9] call for a more detailed examination of the Iliad in at least three of its aspects, which can assist us in understanding its structure and grasping the problem of its creation. These aspects are a) the kinds of lays the Iliad is composed of, b) the battles described and c) the principal epic themes constituting the plot of the poem.

A.   Let us first look at the kinds of lays that make up the Iliad. They are chiefly three: 1) single independent lays, which, in contrast to the epic as a whole, are models of structure and composition;[10] 2) cycles of lays, whose unity and relative independence in relation to the rest of the

---

5.   In the *Diapeira* (II, 73-440) Nestor is unaware of Agamemnon's proposal that they return to Greece; Thersites made the same proposal. It looks as though two versions existed, in each of which a different person made the proposal to return home, and that these versions have been conflated in the Iliad which has reached us.

6.   In IX, alongside the embassy which undertakes to persuade Achilles to return to the war, and which is composed of three people (Ajax, Odysseus and Phoenix), there are traces of a two-man embassy; this is apparent from the use of the dual in lines 182-198. These two versions have certainly been conflated in our Iliad (cf Page 1959, 297f).

7.   On this subject v. Bowra 1930, 87f. The repetitions referred to here are not formulas, eg VI, 46-65; X, 378-381; XI, 131-135; V, 472-492; XVI, 538-545; XVII 142-168.

8.   Bowra 1930, 97f. For example Pylaemenes, who is killed in V, 576, is alive and attending his son's funeral in XIII, 658f. In XV, 63 Zeus promises that Hector shall pursue the Achaeans right up to Achilles' ships, but in XV, 704 Hector pursues the Achaeans as far as Protesilaus' ship. Hector kills Schedius twice and Chromius three times, while in XI 607-609 and XVI 83-86 it appears as if Achilles never received the visit from the Embassy (v. Page 1959, 305. 297f).

9.   Such as the catalogue of the Achaean warriors in II, or scenes like the *Teichoscopia* (Viewing from the Walls) in III, 121-244, or the single-combat between Paris and Menelaus (III, 325f) to settle their differences over Helen, which have nothing to do with the tenth year of the war. Their natural place would be at the beginning of the war.

10.   Such as books I, XVI and XXII, which contain episodes that are of the greatest importance for the whole affair of the Iliad. Other books, like XI and XVIII contain accounts of secondary episodes, and others, like books XVII and XIX, serve simply as padding out. One book, X, is completely intrusive. The length

epic may be clearly distinguished both by their themes and by the beginnings and ends of the cycles;[11] and 3) lays whose only purpose is to serve as connecting links between other longer or shorter, 'independent' parts of the epic.[12]

This diversity in the character of the lays in the Iliad strengthens our doubts both about the unity of its structure and as to whether there was only one poet. It is not possible for all these independent or semi-independent, shorter or longer episodes to have been the work of one person, connected as they are by links which, while keeping to the traditional epic form, are often of a much lower quality. Not even the well-known short preamble to book I, which in effect announces a drama - thus calling for a unity of action - , can unify all this heterogeneous material.

B.   The battles described in the poem also require study. There can be no doubt that the Iliad is a war epic. Nevertheless, for all its thousands of verses and the fifty days' duration of its action, the battles described occupy no more than four days, and of these only two (XI-XVIII and XX-XXI) are given over to the principal theme, the will of Zeus, as it was announced in book I.[13]

It is therefore reasonable to suppose that the first battle we encoun-

of the books varies from 424 (XIX) to 909 (V) lines. The division into books was made by the Alexandrian scholars and is attributed to Zenodotus or Aristarchus. The end of each book coincides with a break in the action of the epic. Individual names have always been given to independent parts of the Homeric epics, even in pre-Alexandrian times (for example cf Herodotus II, 116; Thucydides I 10, 4; Plato's *Republic* I, X, p. 614 B; Aristotle's *Poetica* 16 and 24). And cf Mazon 1967³, 139f; Page 1955, 76.

11.   XX and XXI belong to these cycles, for example. The title, *Theomachy,* suits both of them equally, as does the action, which begins at the beginning of XX and ends in XXI. Other such cycles of lays comprise books XIII+XIV+XV and III+IV+V+VI+VII, even though the latter constitute a synthetic and doubtful unity. Some of these broader unities may very well have consisted originally of smaller fragments, but they look as if they were intended for wider independent recital before they passed into the Iliad.

12.   Here for example all of VIII and a large part of II and VII belong. It must not be forgotten, especially in the case of these books, that their wholly traditional traits put them back in a period of pure oral poetry, and therefore before the middle of the 6th century BC.

13.   On the conventional character of the battles in the Iliad, v. Fenik 1968.

ter (II-VII), and which has no connection with the will of Zeus, is a later addition. It suggests the work of someone who wanted to condense and include in the Iliad the most important events and battles of the nine years of the war that had elapsed before Agamemnon's clash with Achilles. The second battle we meet with in the Iliad (VIII) is also the work of a later poet,[14] who wanted to describe the difficulties which obliged the Achaeans to send Achilles the embassy of book IX. There is, moreover, every reason to believe that the embassy itself is a confused episode, which did not belong to the original Iliad.[15]

Hence the rout of the Achaeans, which was the consequence of Achilles' wrath and withdrawal from the war - and which constitutes a part of the will of Zeus - finally occurs in the third battle, described in XI-XVIII. In this same battle Patroclus is obliged to intervene and is killed, and Achilles decides to take up arms again to avenge the death of his friend.

If the basic material of the Iliad comprised the will of Zeus and the wrath and vengeance of Achilles - as we are told in the beginning of book I - , then it is completely exhausted in books I, XI, XVI and XXII. Nor is it possible to imagine a single unified narration being further expanded. It looks as if this 'basic Iliad' had been expanded later - and expanded considerably - by the incorporation of earlier epic material,[16]

---

14. This is also apparent from the fact that VIII contains very little new, and a great deal of stock material; moreover a four-horse chariot makes its appearance in this book (line 185). Also in VIII there is a clear imitation of Hesiod (lines 15f depend on lines 720 and 811 of the *Theogeny,* and line 443 on line 892 of the *Theogeny*).

15. That our Iliad is based on a version which did not originally include the Embassy episode, is clear from XI, 607-609 and XVI, 83-86; in this connection v. n.6 and Page 1959, 305. 324. 297f. For the rhetorical and therefore later elements in IX, v. Jaeger 1960[2], vol. I, 26f. 40.

16. We have such material in the *aristeia,* for example, and in the exploits of Diomedes in book V, as well as in the description of life at Pylos, the kingdom of the western Peloponnese, which passed into the Iliad by way of loquacious old Nestor (VII, 132; XI, 670 etc.. For the view that the incorporation of this material may have been due to Peisistratus, v. Palmer 1968, 24). We also have such material in the elements coming from Lycian legends, which were incorporated into the Iliad in the persons of Sarpedon, Glaucus and Pandarus (v. Nilsson 1933, 261), as well as in the Catalogue of Ships in book II, which still preserves its prologue (II, 484-487) and in Achilles' Shield in book XVIII. VI

by the conflation of alternative versions of certain episodes[17] and by new additions.[18] This expansion was undoubtedly a long process, carried out over a considerable period of time.

C.   Lastly, it is necessary to examine the principal traditional epic themes composing the Iliad. The four main ones are 1) the Wrath - ἡ μῆνις - of a great hero over an insult he has suffered; 2) Vengeance for the death of a blood relative (or a member of his clan, or a close friend); 3) Reverence for the Old Father; and 4) the *Aristeia,* the single-combat.

The structure of the Iliad and to a large degree its poetical achievement are due to the juxtaposition and interplay of these four main themes. We must nevertheless not forget that each of them has certain basic traditional characteristics, which are respected in the narrative, even if they contradict the basic characteristics of one of the other themes. Let us now look at them more closely:

1)   The Wrath of a great hero over an insult he has received, with which theme in fact the Iliad opens, is perhaps one of the oldest motifs in the epic tradition and illustrates the actual behaviour of the early Achaean warriors. That many examples of such behaviour were known to the ancient Greek world is apparent from Greek mythology and the Homeric epics themselves (Girard 1902, 243; also I, 523f. 553-555; 3,136f; 8, 75f).

constitutes a rather special case. Hector's famous farewell to Andromache is very weakly linked to the rest of the epic; in order to effect this meeting, Hector abandons the battle-field at a very critical moment, when his presence was vitally needed, to take an unimportant message to his mother, which could have been sent by any ordinary messenger; and then, although this is supposed to be Hector's and Andromache's final farewell, in VII, 310 we find Hector returning to Troy and sleeping, indeed, in his own house (381 and 477). Wilamowitz expressed the opinion that this famous scene came from some *Hectoreis.* v. also Murray 1937[3], chap. IX.

17.   eg the *Diapeira* or the Embassy (v. n.5 and 6).. Also the exchange of Achilles' and Patroclus' arms in XVI. On this v. Wilamowitz 1920, 116f.
18.   Such are book X (which not even antiquity considered to be a genuine part of the Iliad. cf. Il. Schol. I at the beginning of X), the games at Patroclus' funeral in XXIII, and above all book XXIV, with which the Iliad ends. cf Kirk 1962, 320f. For XXIV v. Leaf 1902[2], 536.
19.   I call them 'traditional' because they are frequently found in the epics in more expanded or more compressed forms.

The unquenchable wrath of the warrior who has been insulted is
connected with the heroic sense of *arete*, valour in battle, and the
fighter's demand to be honoured by his peers. Like the gods, the heroes
of that ancient society demanded to be honoured for their might, and
were always ready to punish whoever opposed their will or dared to dishonour them.

In the original form of the primitive heroic code of conduct,
amends could only be made in the same coin - humiliation for humiliation.
That is the attitude of Ajax, for example, who, maddened by his dishonour, even in Hades maintains his hatred for Odysseus undiminished
(11, 541). And Thetis asks Zeus to pay back Agamemnon in the same
kind for the insult he offered her son. Achilles is demanding the same
thing when he tells the envoys sent to him by the Achaeans that
Agamemnon will never persuade him to take part again in the battle:

"First he must pay me in kind for the bitter humiliation I
endured." (IX, 387)

Later, other forms of restitution were permitted by the heroic code
and the Greek penal code [20] (Jones 1956, 257; Wolf 1946, 31f). This
change is apparent in Iliad IX and XIX, and especially from Phoenix's
words, when he is trying to persuade Achilles to accept Agamemnon's
gifts and join the battle again:

"We have heard many comparable tales of noblemen in olden times,
who had worked themselves up into a passion, yet proved amenable
to gifts and yielded to persuasion." (IX, 524-526).

In the Iliad Achilles eventually gives in and returns to the war without obtaining full satisfaction 'in kind'. Nevertheless it is not the royal gifts
that persuade him to lay aside his wrath, in spite of the fact that he also
does incidentally accept them in XIX,[21] but the death of Patroclus, his
closest friend.

---

20. Restitution by 'payment', or a forfeit, instead of by blood and vengeance,
    appears only twice in the Iliad - in XVIII, 497-508 and IX, 632-636. Both
    these instances are justly considered to be later additions.
21. In XIX we appear to have yet another conflation of two versions: in the later
    one the wrath of Achilles ends with the acceptance of the gifts promised him
    by Agamemnon, and not with the death of Patroclus; in the earlier one

2)   This brings us to the second of the principal epic themes in the Iliad, Vengeance for the death of a relative (or a member of the household, or a close friend).

It is particularly significant that in the Iliad we often find two brothers (or paternal half-brothers) or even first cousins (paternal again) fighting side by side on foot or from a chariot, the one as driver and the other as *paraibates*. This combination is not just limited to the race of men; we also find examples among demi-gods, rivers and even gods (Trypanis 1963, 289f).

When an epic motif recurrs as often as it does in the case of relatives up to the first degree of cousinhood (μέχρις ἀνεψιότητος) who fight to-gather as a pair, it is reasonable to conclude that it represents some historical fact. It would seem then that this pairing was part of the earliest military organization of the Achaeans, and that it derived from the primitive duty of kinsmen to support each other, to avenge their murdered relative and to take care of his burial.[22]

The custom of kinsmen fighting together, which was transferred from warriors fighting on foot to warriors fighting with chariots, required, as we have seen, the same kinship bond between driver and *paraibates*.[23] The warrior had to rely absolutely on his driver, to be certain that he would rescue him if he fell wounded, and that he would ensure his burial should he receive a mortal blow. In that ancient time this absolute confidence could only be guaranteed by blood ties and the duty imposed by kinship, and not by military discipline, which was a later development.

Achilles returns to the war because of Patroclus' death. Yet when Achilles enumerates the evil consequences of his wrath (XIX, 56f), he makes no mention of Patroclus' death; nor is there any reference to it in Agamemnon's reply (XIX, 146f). In lines 210f, however, Patroclus' death is taken as understood.

22.   v. Lipsius 1905-1912 II, 2, 552f; also Latte 1931, 32 and Bury 1951, 53f. This is where the fierce battle fought over the body of a kinsman has its roots. v. XIV, 449f; XVII, 346f. and v. Bethe 1927 III, 299f.

It must not be forgotten that they expelled from the clan not only the man guilty of the murder, but also the man who failed to avenge a kinsman's death. v. Glotz 1904, 34.

23.   Evidence for these related pairs of warriors may be seen in the dual form Αἴαντε, which signifies Ajax and his brother. Ajax in our Iliad, of course, always fights on foot. v. Page 1959, 236.

Another ancient custom linked to the epic theme under discussion was that of receiving into a home the suppliant who had left his country because of some crime committed, especially murder.[24] The suppliants apparently enjoyed the rights, but also shared the duties, of the new clan which offered them the shelter of its roof (Busolt 1920, 954).

The most important 'suppliant' in the Iliad is unquestionably Patroclus. According to the myth, while still a child he had accidentally killed the son of Amphidamas. This murder obliged him to leave his country and take refuge in Phthia, where Peleus received him into his house-hold and brought him up with every devotion (ἐνδυκέως), (XXIII, 82f). Later Patroclus took part in the Trojan campaign at Achilles' side.

At some early stage in the epic tradition Patroclus was probably Achilles' charioteer;[25] as we have seen, the Achaeans entrusted this duty only to kinsmen (or members of the same household). This, along with the fact that Patroclus and Achilles were deemed able to share a common grave,[26] supports the view that in the original version Patroclus shared in the rights and duties of the clan, of Achilles' household, and, before all else, in the suppliant's right to claim protection as well as vengeance and an honoured burial if he were killed. I believe that this constituted the original version (and the central core) of Achilles' fierce desire to avenge Patroclus' death: it was a deep religious duty, the neglect of which would have had direct consequences for the honour of the hero and all his clan. That was the only motivation powerful enough to make Achilles put aside the insult he had received and shake off his stubborn private wrath.

---

24. We find many such suppliants in the Homeric epics, such as Phoenix (IX, 478f), Epigeus (XVI, 570), Lycophron (XV, 437f), or Medon (XV, 333f). cf also 14, 379f; 15, 223f, etc. . The fact that in XXIV, 480f the suppliant murderer is used as one part of a simile is an indication of how common this phenomenon was.
25. The fact that the epithets ἱππεῦ and ἱπποκέλευθε, which are applied to Patroclus, are not found in any other Greek text, reinforces this supposition; cf XVII 426f, XVII, 475f, XXIII, 280f and v. also Page 1959, 286, n. 90; E. Ebeling 1880-1885 under Πάτροκλος.
26. cf XXIII, 243f; 24, 76f. This must not be confused with the exceptional instances, known from historical times, when many warriors were buried in a common grave or communal tomb, as at Marathon, Thermopylae and Plateia.

In time this motive seems to have been forgotten, when in later stages of Greek history the 'companies' (ἑταιρεῖαι) appeared; these were associations of men of the same age and social class, bound by an oath of mutual assistance in times of peace as well as war (Latte 1931, 32f). And when the companions, (ἑταῖροι) the members of these companies, were brought into the epic tradition, their rights and duties became confused with those of blood relatives, so that gradually the new relationships came to hide the old ones. Thus Achilles and Patroclus, who shared no true kinship, were at first regarded as ἑταῖροι, companions, and later simply as close friends;[27] they had ceased to be thought of as two men bound together by common clan and household rights and obligations. Later still, in Classical and Hellenistic times, they came to be thought of as a pair of lovers, [28] for the very reason that posterity interpreted Achilles' devotion in terms of its own emotions. [29]

However, in order to comprehend the fierce passion with which Achilles seeks to avenge Patroclus' death and bestow the proper honours on his corpse, we must delve more deeply into the roots of this epic theme, back to the stern primitive duty of the clan or household to avenge the death of a kinsman; this was the only duty with the power to bend a hero like Achilles and force him to lay aside his personal anger and return to battle. That later generations modified or interpreted this theme in a different manner, in order to adapt it to their own notions of comradeship or friendship, is due to the shifting character of this long-lived epic tradition out of which the Iliad and Odyssey were born.

Finally, I should like to emphasize that the Vengeance of Achilles in the Iliad possesses the power and beauty which it does because most of the descriptions connected with the theme are concerned with events that took place after Patroclus' death. In this way a special tragic and

27. Two other close friends, but on the Trojan side, are Glaucus and Sarpedon. Their friendship, which constitutes a later addition to the Trojan cycle, is modelled on that of Achilles and Patroclus.
28. This is how Aeschylus interpreted the friendship of Achilles and Patroclus in the *Myrmidons.* cf Schmid - Stählin 1929 I, 1, 63, n. 8.
29. Could it be that the same household nucleus is also found in another similar friendship in Greek mythology, that of Orestes and Pylades ? Orestes was also a fugitive who found asylum with, and was brought up under the same roof as Pylades.

romantic touch is added, which would not be present had most of the scenes occurred while both friends were still alive. Because everything is enacted in retrospect, it has the remote, fugitive beauty lent by distance and irretrievability. Whatever Achilles may do, whether he kills Hector and dishonours his body, or honours Patroclus with the most magnificent burial and most splendid burial games, he cannot restore him to life. And furthermore, these honours all have a certain special pathos because they are being paid to his dead friend by a young warrior who is himself condemned to die so soon.

Before proceeding to the third basic epic theme in the Iliad, we must pause briefly to consider the mutual interaction of the first two, the Wrath and the Vengeance motifs. The combination of these two elements gives the whole epic its tragic depth and constitutes its chief originality. The poet of the original Iliad, by presenting Patroclus as also a victim of this same wrath of Achilles, renders Achilles' anguish all the sharper and his passion for vengeance all the more furious (Mazon 1942, 243), quite apart from any moral or sacred obligation imposed by kinship or friendship.

3)   The third epic theme in the Iliad is that of the Old Father, which is developed in XXIV, where it is also combined with the equally ancient epic theme of the Suppliant. [30]

Youth and manly vigour are projected in the Iliad against a background not only of death - natural enough in poetry about war - but also of old age. Here once again contrast is used to give emphasis to the lustre of beauty and youth.

For this purpose the person of the old father [31] is employed in the epic, a figure of great lyric and tragic importance in ancient Greek poetry. This is no doubt due to the status of the *pater familias* in Greek society,

---

30.   The Suppliant theme is commoner in the Iliad than in the Odyssey. Such suppliants are, for example, the suppliant-murderers of whom we spoke in the theme of close friendship.

31.   The portrayal of the father as old - and in fact very old - is a stock component of epic tradition. Peleus, for instance, is on the threshold of death (cf XI, 771. 782; XIX, 336f; XVIII, 434-435), while Achilles has barely passed his twentieth year and Peleus himself, according to the myth, had been young when he married Thetis.

in which originally the father had the right of life and death over the members of his household.

There are many instances of the use of the Old Father theme in the Iliad, sometimes in a more, sometimes in a less developed form,[32] until in XXIV it becomes the principal theme of that book and determines the conclusion of the epic. Here, as in the case of Chryses in I, the Old Father motif is combined with the equally old and important epic theme of the Suppliant, thus acquiring greater pathos and richness of colour.

It could be said, then, that in Iliad XXIV the protagonist is no longer Achilles but Priam, and that its author - a great poet indeed - even uses the traditional Old Father theme (combined in this instance with the Suppliant theme) with special reference to Achilles. That invincible and pitiless warrior must also bow to the demands of this epic theme: he must honour the aged father and be defeated by him, just as in book I Agamemnon, the all-powerful king, had to honour the old suppliant-father Chryses and was defeated by him.

It should be observed that in the tragic meeting between Priam and Achilles the scene opens with a reference to the Old Father theme:

"Most worshipful Achilles, think of your own father, who is the same age as I, and so has nothing but miserable old age ahead of him," (XXIV, 486-487)

says Priam, as he falls at Achilles' feet. And when he has finished his moving speech, Achilles is reminded again of his elderly father and the situation Priam now finds himself in: an old father who has done what no man has ever done before, kissed the hand of the man who killed his sons.

And the magnificent description continues. In Achilles' dimly lit

---

32. Thus the whole Iliad begins with the Old Father theme, when in book I Chryses, an old father who is also a suppliant, brings down a plague on the Achaeans with his curse. Other old fathers in the Iliad are: Aeneas' father (XVII, 323f), Pandarus' father, Lycaon (V, 197f), Phegeus' and Idaeus' father, Dares (V, 10-24), Nestor's father, Neleus (XI, 696), Nestor himself (XXIII, 615), Abas' and Polyidus' father, Eurydamas (V, 148), Xanthus' and Thoon's father, Phaenops (V, 152f), Priam (XXII, 33f. 410f) and Laertes (24, 225f). Even Polyctor, the hypothetical father of the disguised Hermes, is old (XXIV, 397).

18

tent both men, overcome by their memories, give rein to their emotions; Priam, still lying at Achilles' feet, laments with bitter tears the man-slaying Hector, and Achilles, motionless, first laments for his old and feeble father who is so soon to lose his only son, and then for Patroclus - whom he now knows he will have to 'betray' by handing back Hector's body to be buried.

As soon as they are both recovered a little from their anguish, Achilles rises to his feet and, out of pity for Priam's white hair, takes him by the hand, sits him down and speaks to him of the past happy life and the present sorrow of the old king. Then his duty as a host and his compassion for the death-ridden father constrain him to offer Priam hospitality; he gives him food and puts him to sleep in the portico - which is where in the epics' guests usually sleep - and there Hermes comes to him and leads him back to Troy together with Hector's body.

Thus although the Iliad begins with the trials and horror provoked by the dishonouring of the old father Chryses, it ends with a strange sense of tranquility and appeasement, as proper honour is paid to the old father Priam in the final stage of development attained by this epic theme in XXIV. [33] It is also worth noting (this is the first example of it) that it is from here that European humanism takes its beginning.

We should further point out that what heightens the tragedy and reveals the whole intensity of the father's devotion, and Hector's worth as well, is the fact that here alone in all the Greek epic tradition ransom is paid for a dead and not a living man. [34]

Thus the old father, for all that his limbs are now feeble, is presented as stronger than all the stalwart warriors of Troy, none of whom

---

33. It is worthy of note that Priam's words, "λυσόμενος παρὰ σεῖο, φέρω δ' ἀπερείσι ἄποινα (XXIV, 502) echo line I, 13 referring to Chryses, "λυσόμενός τε θύγατρα φέρων τ'ἀπερείσι' ἄποινα". cf Sheppard 1922, 208.

34. This also is evidence that book XXIV is late, and that it was completed at a time when heroic wars and their customs were already forgotten. Ransom for a living captive is, of course, another matter (cf VI, 45f; X, 378f; XI, 122f; XI, 131f; XXII, 41f). For the late date of XXIV v. Schmid - Stählin 1929 l.c. and the lines XXIV, 397f, in which recruitment by lot is mentioned, and Monro 1957[4], note on XXIV, 400. More particularly v. Kirk 1962, 320f and Leaf 1902[2], 536.

would have been able to save Hector's corpse from the dogs and vultures. Consequently the Iliad in its conclusion constitutes not only a triumphant monument to youth and manly prowess, as has so often been pointed out, but a monument to old age, moral courage, devotion and wisdom. Sometimes the weapons of age are stronger than all the weapons of youth in its prime - and that is a lesson which our own era should not forget. [35]

4)   The last of the basic traditional themes in the Iliad that we shall examine is the *Aristeia,* the single-combat.

The description of a single-combat possesses certain natural poetic attractions which have ensured its place and growth in epic tradition. [36] A single-combat creates more interest than the description of a crowded battle, because it emphasizes the individual element. This is the reason we find many writers breaking up crowded battle scenes into smaller episodes, in which the role of the individual is more clearly prominent, thus enhancing the human interest and increasing the poetic power.

Single-combats occupy an important place in the Iliad, because they reflect the highest ideals of epic poetry. They are independent scenes, which sometimes seem to have been taken from other epics and which often have only a very loose connection with the main thread of events. Such are the single-combats between Menelaus and Paris (III), Diomedes (V), Hector and Ajax (VII), Agamemnon and Hector (XI), Patroclus and Sarpedon (XVI) and many others of lesser importance. They all indeed converge on the preparation for the great *aristeia* - which is also the central episode of the whole epic - of the single-combat between Achilles and Hector in XXII. [37] In every *aristeia* valour is displayed by both sides, as is natural, since victory only has worth when the opponent is important and worthy of the victor.

---

35. On this subject, cf the position held by Nestor in the epics. Also v. Quintus Smyrnaeus V, 155-156.
36. The importance of the *aristeia* theme is further illustrated by the fact that we also find it in scenes in which the gods play the leading roles (eg in XXI, 383f).
37. Single-combats with axes sometimes occur in the Iliad (XIII, 600f, in which Menelaus and Peisander do battle), and even with huge stones (VII, 265f). Both these forms are evidence of primitive ways of fighting.

Every time a warrior is killed a battle ensues over the body, because his kinsmen and fellow warriors cannot allow the enemy to carry it off, strip it of its arms and throw it to the dogs and vultures. They must do their utmost to ensure him a proper burial.

This epic theme of the Battle over the Body of the Dead Warrior is naturally frequently encountered in the Iliad; it is not, however, developed fully except in the great battle over the body of Patroclus (XVII), the narration of which is like an extension of the description of his death, and an additional method of emphasizing the hero's worth; the greater the hero who is slain, the fiercer the struggle over his body - that is the way epic tradition wants it.

Since the less important single-combats are numerous in the Iliad, it is natural that variety was sought in the manner in which they were presented. In one case the psychology of the hero is described in detail, in another there is greater emphasis on the list of the enemies he has killed - the longer the list, the more important the hero (a very primitive form of description. Lesky 1966, 53f). And again, both in the taunts exchanged before a battle and in the boasting over the dead body, different allusions are made to the hero's country, clan and life.

Besides all this, many realistic details are given about the parts of the body where the warrior was struck and the way in which he was killed. On only one occasion is the single-combat used to introduce the theme of reconciliation; and this is brilliantly developed in the famous scene between Glaucus and Diomedes (VI, 119f).

Nevertheless all the single-combats, both those treated at length and those mentioned more briefly, lead up to the great *aristeia* of Achilles and Hector in XXII. This is the culmination of the Vengeance theme as well as being the crowning point of the whole epic, as Virgil well understood when he took it as a model for the single-combat between Aeneas and Turnus in the Aeneid. Furthermore, book XXII is the crowning point of the Iliad, because everything that has gone before is a preparation for it, and because it sets the scene for the ending, the finale of the work. This is also apparently why, in the final Iliad, all the other important single-combats (with the sole exception of the *aristeia* of Patroclus and Sarpedon [38]) are cut short and left uncompleted. A human, or a god, or the night intervenes and stops them; the reason is that if they were given in full, they would diminish the impact made by the final confrontation between Achilles and Hector.

This tragic encounter of the two great heroes takes place under the walls of Troy, in front of all the Trojans and Achaeans, and it is more than just a conventional single-combat. [39] It is something out of the ordinary, just as the two heroes taking part in it are out of the ordinary. The outcome will decide the fate not only of the two adversaries, but of all the Trojans and Achaeans. Hector's death will not only be Achilles' vengeance for the death of Patroclus; it will be tantamount to the destruction of Troy and the vengeance of Menelaus for the insult he received when Paris carried Helen off. It will at the same time, however, be tantamount to Achilles' own death, and it is this that gives the tragic tone to the hero's greatest triumph. For Achilles knows - he has been many times forewarned - that he is doomed to die himself within a short time after he has killed Hector. [40]

These four main epic themes - Wrath, Vengeance, the Old Father and the Single-combat - form the backbone of the Iliad. We can follow the basic outline in books I, XI, XVI, XXII and XXIV. They are not, of course, the only epic themes employed, but all the others play a much smaller part in the basic structure of the work.

However, in the course of epic tradition, these four themes (which were originally only three, since it looks as though the Old Father episode in XXIV is a later addition; v. 18f) were expanded, as we have said, so that the Iliad developed into something much broader in scope

---

38. This *aristeia* is considered by many scholars to be late, and influenced in many respects by the single-combat between Achilles and Hector in XXII.
39. It is obvious that some reworking of the single-combat between Achilles and Hector went on as epic tradition advanced. This is apparent from the primitive elements contained in it (eg XXII, 371f), from the weapons used by Achilles (above all by the μελίη, the traditional thrusting-spear, which was not used for throwing, although in our Iliad Achilles hurls it at Hector; and also from the two Geometric casting-spears which are a later type of weapon), and from the appearance of Athena in the guise of Deiphobus, etc. .
40. The shadow of death lies over Achilles from the very beginning of the epic. cf I, 416; XVIII, 95-96; XIX, 408. 416; XXI, 110; XXII, 358.

than just an account of the events taking place during the fifty days encompassed by its action.

Thus we learn of the cause which led to the Trojan war: Paris' abduction of Helen. We are given a catalogue of the heroes who took part in it. We hear about the leaders of the Achaeans, about Diomedes, the two Ajaxes, Idomeneus, Odysseus; and about the leaders of the Trojans and their allies. We see Paris, the chief culprit, and Menelaus fight in single-combat. We follow the exploits of Diomedes, and we can look behind the walls of Troy and see Priam and the Trojan leaders watching the Achaean army, and, then, Andromache and her son taking leave of Hector. In this way many elements from the prehistory of the Iliad are included in the epic, as well as much that happened after its end.

It is quite natural that most of this heterogeneous matter passed into the Iliad as padding out of the Wrath theme, because the interval between Achilles' refusal to fight (I) and his giving Patroclus leave to go to the help of the Achaeans (XI) afforded various rhapsodes the opportunity of filling the gap with a heap of episodes, many of which were unrelated to the rest of the epic. For this reason we need not be surprised to find lighter and often amusing episodes in the first half of the Iliad, which add a touch very different from the serious and tragic spirit of the final books.

For example the maltreatment of Thersites (II), the unheroic flight of Paris to the arms of Helen (III), the foolish credulity of Pandarus (IV), Ares' bellowing (V), Aphrodite's tears when she is wounded by Diomedes (V) are humourous episodes, and in direct contrast to the dark, heavy turn taken by the narrative thereafter (although this does not hold true for the scenes with the gods).

It is unnecessary to point out that such padding was also added to the Vengeance theme, with the result that the whole work came to acquire a curious concertina-like form. The Iliad can be characterized as a drama with retardations, which become shorter in length as the action approaches its conclusion, but which are also liable to every sort of expansion or abbreviation, according to the requirements of the recitation. [41]

41. I should like to add here the excellent outline given by Professor E. Dodds in

Whether this outside material was added gradually to the Iliad as a consequence of the technique itself of oral poetry (which, we have seen, modifies the poem and adds fresh material at each new recitation), or whether all the additions were made in the course of the final monumental composition of the work, is something we cannot know. At all events, I believe that the parts of the Iliad attributable to the final monumental composition are those which clearly show that they were once independent lays, such as the Catalogue of the Ships[42] (II), Hector's Discourse with Andromache (VI), the *Doloneia* (X), the description of Achilles' Shield (XVIII) (Bethe 1914, 90. 91 n 8; Wilamowitz 1920, 163f; Cauer 1921, 658), as well as certain abridgements, or conflations of two different variations of the same episode, like the Testing (II) or the Embassy (IX). To the final composition must also belong such feeble balancing-out additions as the Catalogue of the Trojans (II, 816-877), or the description of the 'other weapons' made for Achilles by Hephaestus[43] (XVIII).

There are also certain other 'variations' in the text of the Iliad, whose provenance appears to be later still, and which perhaps derive from the 'books of the rhapsodes', which appeared after the composition of the monumental Iliad was committed to writing: they were useful to the rhapsodes, who thus had at their disposal the different versions of various passages some of which later became incorporated, one alongside another, in the text we have today. Here for example, probably belong the two alternative similes describing the Achaeans setting out for Troy[44] (II), or the two similes in XI (548f and 558f), in which Ajax is compared first with a lion and then with an ass being beaten by boys with sticks. Naturally there are also still later interpolations incorporated into the present text.[45]

------

his lectures on the Iliad at Oxford, which I had the good fortune to attend: Act I: book I - Retardation: books II - X. Act II: book XI - Retardation: books XII - XV, 591. Act III: books XV, 592 - XIX - Retardation: the greater part of books XX - XXI. Act IV: books XXII - XXIII, 256 - Retardation: book XXIII, 257 to the end of XXIII. Act V: book XXIV.

42. For the Catalogue of Ships and its origins, v. the opposing views of Heubeck 1949, 197; 1957, 40; 1961, 116; Page 1959, 118f.; Webster 1958, 132. 175.
43. These weak lines (XVIII, 610-613) had already been obelized by Aristarchus.
44. Lines II, 459-468 and II, 469-473 are alternatives for lines II, 455-458. After lines 457-458 they are out of place.
45. Such interpolations are lines VIII, 73-74; IX, 320. 382-384. 616; X11, 175 - 180; XX, 269-272. 332-334.

Our knowledge about the first stages in the development of the Greek epic is so limited, that no positive answer can be given to the question, whether the basic plot of the Iliad is original, or whether the epic drew on earlier sources. The very ancient, traditional character of the Wrath theme makes it unnecessary to assume that the Wrath of Achilles must proceed from the older Wrath of Meleager.[46] And there is no clear indication that the *Aethiopis,* an epic poem which presents Achilles fighting against the Aethiopian prince, Memnon, had any influence on the *aristeia* of Achilles and Hector in the Iliad.[47] We do not know to what period the original *Aethiopis* belongs, and it seems much more likely that the Iliad influenced its development than the reverse.

Nor furthermore can the question, whether the Iliad is based on an actual Mycenean campaign against Troy, help to solve the problem of the Iliad's originality (Page 1959, 971; Hampl 1962, 37; Finley et al. 1964, 1f). It is possible that real historical events do lie behind the Iliad; but so many changes have taken place within the epic tradition that it is impossible to say for certain whether they had any substantial influence on the structure of the poem (Lesky 1967, 1202).

Another important problem is the length of the Iliad, which even in antiquity was proverbial (Aeschines, *Against Ctesiphon* 100; Cicero, *Ad Atticum,* VIII, 11). Its great length immediately poses the question, for what audience was an epic of 15, 693 lines intended (Murray 1937[3], 187; Page 1955, 75 n8) ? Three days of continuous recital are required to finish the poem. At a festival or in the agora no one would have been able to hold the same audience for three whole days,[48] any more than

---

46. The view that the Iliad owes much to an older *Meleagreia* was expressed by I. T. Kakrides (1949, 11f).
47. For the influence of the *Aethiopis* on the Iliad, v. Schadewaldt (1959[3], 155). It is not impossible that the construction of Memnon's shield by Hephaestus and the Weighing of the Souls in the *Little Iliad* are due to the influence of the Iliad. It is also quite possible, however, that the weighing of the souls was one of the traditional epic themes (cf XVI, 658). For a probable mutual-interraction between the Iliad and the *Aethiopis* in the period of oral transmission, cf Fenik 1968, 239f.
48. Even at festivals lasting many days, such as the Delia on Delos or the Panionia at Mycale, no rhapsode could have hoped to hold the same audience for three whole days running, when there were so many other interesting things to watch

it would have been possible to recite such a huge work at smaller gatherings, for example weddings, banquets or funerals.

Furthermore the structure of the Iliad also precludes its recital by instalments: first, because it does not contain episodes of equal length, suitable for reciting in parts [49] ; and second, because, as we have seen, it contains long passages which only serve as links to connect independent episodes of unequal length. Such long - and not particularly interesting - bridging passages would only hinder its recital in parts. The same reason precludes the recital of the epic in its entirety for days on end at the court of some king, tryant or ruler.[50]

Nor again was the monumental composition of the Iliad intended for a reading public, because such a public did not exist before the 6th century in Greece, even though writing and the Greek alphabet were already widely diffused by then.

Thus we find ourselves faced with the phenomenon of a great epic which has been carefully assembled, without the poet or poets who gave it its monumental form having in mind any actual audience that could enjoy it in its entirety - a most paradoxical phenomenon in the history of literature!

and listen to - boxing, dancing, singing, etc. (cf the Homeric *Hymn to Delian Apollo*). Nor have we any ancient evidence to the effect that the recital of the epics was performed by instalments. Moreover, at the festivals of the Panathenaea from the 6th century on, ancient sources tell us that the Homeric epics were to be exclusively recited, and in their correct order, and that each rhapsode had to begin where the previous one left off. Therefore the contests between the rhapsodes must have been in the recitation of sections of the Iliad or Odyssey. v. Lycurgus, *Contra Leocr.* 102; Pseudo-Plato - *Hipparchus* 228 B, and Diogenes Laertius I, 2, 57. All three sources seem to agree. v. also Mazon 1967[3], 234 n. 4.

49. The end of every Homeric book coincides with a break in the action. But no scholar to date has been able to show how the epic could be broken up into consecutive instalments of roughly equal length.

50. Insofar as a long poem is not constructed in such a way as to allow the separate recital of its different parts, it is natural to suppose that it never was recited in this manner. But cf Wade-Gery 1952, 14. Bards permanently resident in a royal palace, as described in the Odyssey, are inconceivable in the context of the Greek Dark Age which followed the Mycenean period.

Now let us turn to the creator or creators of the monumental Iliad. This question suggests three main possibilities, of which the last is perhaps also the most probable.

1.   We could suppose that the Iliad was composed by the group which, it is said, Peisistratus commissioned to collect the Homeric poems and put them "in their proper order", so that they could be recited at the Panathenaea.[48] This would explain the loose structure of the work and, to a great extent, the heterogeneous material which, as we have seen, was included in it. On the other hand the very few Attic elements to be found in the Homeric text argue against this theory. If the Peisistratan rhapsodes were the creators of the monumental Iliad, then we ought to find many more atticisms in the text as well as many elements of the post-oral poetic period and technique - elements of style, vocabulary, concepts. These are in fact very few.

2.   We could also attribute the monumental Iliad to some Ionic guild of rhapsodes, like the Homeridae of Chios. We could say that during the 7th century they had collected a large amount of the Trojan epic material which was then circulating in the Ionian world, and with it they created the rambling Iliad with its loose composition that we have today. It has also been suggested (Mazon 1967³ 258f) that the basis for this work was an older, much shorter and more closely knit Iliad, the general outline of which can perhaps still be detected today beneath the huge unified edifice constructed by these Ionian rhapsodes. In any case this monumental creation, our own Iliad, would not have been intended to be recited all at one time. Its purpose would have been to serve as a fund of epic poetry from which the rhapsodes could draw passages for recital according to the requirements of the situation.

Something of the sort is certainly not impossible, because guilds of rhapsodes, as we have seen, did exist, and the anomalous structure of the Iliad lends support to the view that some shabby editorial work may have taken place in the Archaic period - at the end of the 8th or beginning of the 7th century - for even those parts of the epic which connect the different episodes or reshape parallel versions clearly display the characteristics of a living epic tradition. Against this view militates the fact that there is no necessity, poetic or otherwise, to postulate any such joint composition by a school of rhapsodes, and we have no other comparable example from Greece of the 8th or early 7th century.

3.   We can assume that the monumental Iliad is the work of one man - and this seems to be the most likely hypothesis. The gifted rhapsode who composed it used in the ambitious monumental creation fragments of his Trojan repertoire as well as much other earlier material. There were of course many ways in which these elements could have been combined, which is why it is dangerous to differentiate between and to attribute - as Wilamowitz and other scholars have done - different passages of the Iliad to earlier bards, or to maintain that particular parts have been subject to earlier elaboration (Wilamowitz 1920, 26f).

It has been justly said (Kirk 1962, 316f) that such a leap from the 'great' to the 'monumental' work accords better with the ambition, abilities and reputation of one individual than with the collective effort of some school. A parallel which gives some support to this contention may be found in the manufacture of the huge Geometric amphorae or craters, some of which are seven feet high and larger than any previous vases.

In any case, what can be completely excluded is the notion that the Iliad consists of a simple, random conglomeration of Trojan material. The pure overall design of the epic, the frequent allusions from one part of the work to another and the obvious bridging passages completely eliminate such a hypothesis.

Unfortunately an analysis of the Iliad's structure throws no further light on the person of Homer (v. 1f), nor on the role he might have played in the composition of this vast epic. It is however clear that the Iliad in its totality is not the work of one poet, so we can also exclude the old belief which held that the whole of the Iliad - virtually every line of it - was the work of Homer.

Various theories about Homer's role in this epic have been put forward. The 'nucleus theory' in its original form placed Homer at the beginning of a long line of evolution leading up to the final shaping of the Iliad. Against this theory it has been correctly objected, first, that the style and language of the Iliad, even in the 'earlier' parts, have a technical perfection that presupposes the existence of a long epic tradition; and second, that a large part of the contents of the Iliad consists of traditional myths and legends which must have had an extended existence before the narrative of the Wrath of Achilles took shape.

Wilamowitz (1920) tried to get round these objections by proposing the view that Homer should be placed not at the beginning but in the middle of the long tradition from which the Iliad came: in other words, that he lived in Chios in the 8th century and that he took over the work of the pre-Homeric poets, stitched it together and gave it a design. The work of Homer himself, according to Wilamowitz, was later expanded and partly remodelled by a series of subsequent post-Homeric rhapsodes.

The dating of Homer to the 8th century received wide acceptance among Unitarians and Analysts alike,[51] but it still remains no more than the simple hypothesis of a great scholar, based only on indirect evidence.

The one certain fact - which we have already stressed - is that Homer lived before the 7th century; but how long before, we unfortunately do not know (v. 1f). We can also say with some assurance that Homer was a gifted rhapsode from Ionia, whose repertory included the Iliad; but which, and how large, those parts of the Iliad that constitute his original creation, what has been reworked and what added to the epic, or even whether he was the sole creator of the monumental work - these are questions to which no sure answers can be given.

We should also add that there is considerable evidence, linguistic and otherwise,[52] confirming that the Iliad in its later stages, as well as in its final monumental form, was a product of Ionia. And this evidence agrees with the indications we have that Homer was of Ionian birth.

---

51. Fifty years before, a much older chronology was fashionable. W. Leaf, Sir Richard Jebb, J. B. Bury and Sir William Ridgeway placed the earlier parts of the Iliad in about the 11th century BC.
52. Thus 1) cremation, which we find in the Iliad, was the commonest form of burial in Ionia from the 9th to the 7th century, as is clear from the Geometric graves of Colophon, while at Mycenae the bodies were buried in shaft-graves or tholos tombs (cf Mylonas 1948, 56f). 2) The absence of any element of hero-cult in the Iliad is also an Ionian trait. 3) In the similes the west and north winds blow from off the sea (IV, 275. 422; XIV, 395) or from Thrace (IX,5). 4) All the geographical place names which can be determined are Ionian; the

If then the Iliad was a monumental composition, modelled after the principles and needs of oral poetry, when was it written down for the first time? The Mycenean script was probably never used for epic poetry in the Mycenean period, and during the course of the Greek Dark Age illiteracy reigned in Greece. Consequently anything relating to written epic poetry can only be traced back as far as the 8th century and after, in other words, the period following the dissemination of the Greek alphabet.

It is therefore probable that the Iliad was committed to writing at the time of its 'monumental' composition, or nearly so, around the end of the 8th century. For if it had been transmitted during the 7th century only orally, we should find palpable signs of that century in the text; poetic, and other concepts and ideas of the 7th century would have crept into the epic. In addition that century would have left its traces in the language of the Iliad, quite apart from how accurate the 7th century oral singers may have been, or the aura that may have surrounded the Iliad as being something unique in the epic tradition (cf Bowra 1955, 9f). If, again, the written version had been made in the 6th century, at the time of Peisistratus, the technique and style of written verse would certainly have diminished the purity, facility and simplicity of the formulae, which are exclusively characteristic of oral composition (Kirk 1962, 95f).

I fear, however, that we shall never know whether in fact the poet who composed the Iliad is also the one who wrote it down, or whether an illiterate and perhaps blind rhapsode, as tradition has it, dictated it to some scribe, who wrote it down for the first time. Unfortunately no contemporary analogy can aid us in the solution of this problem, because we do not know in what way the advent of writing at the end of the 8th century influenced the Ionian rhapsodes.[53]

However that may be, it was the creator - or creators - of this 'monumental' Iliad who created the 'great epic' for Greece and for all

Icarian sea (II, 144), the meadows of Caystrus (II, 461); cf also Niobe on Sipylus (XXIV 614f). The lines XXIII, 227 and XXIV, 13 cannot be taken as contrary evidence because they do not say that the dawn rises out of the sea, but that it spreads across the sea.

53. Interesting views have been expressed by, among others, D. L. Page (1959, 158), who places Homer around the 9th century, and Adam Parry (1966, 201).

the western world (Wilamowitz 1927b, 12).

Now that we have examined some of the basic problems concerning the composition of the Iliad, it is only right to add that its extraordinary poetic achievement is largely due to the structure itself, in other words to the dramatic manner in which different episodes are presented. For the destinies of Achilles and Hector not only justify but invite comparison with Greek tragedy, by reason of the dramatic manner in which the events are set down.[54]

In place of a smooth, uniform flow and a leisurely epic narration of events, the Iliad displays a purely dramatic construction, which concentrates the action around a few principal characters and incidents, and abounds in cross-references. Hence if we pick our way through all the different stages of the plot - the plot of a work with only heroes, and no villains - we finally arrive at the epic's tragic culmination, and it differs entirely from the ending of any other great heroic poem. Because Achilles feels no joy when he has vanquished Hector; the Iliad ends with the inconsolable grief of its central hero, with the laments of the Greeks for Patroclus and of the Trojans for Hector, and with the heavy shadow of death, so soon to strike Achilles down.

The Structure of the Odyssey.

If the Iliad can be characterized as a drama with retardations, with heroes but without villains, it may be said of the Odyssey that it is an adventure story with both good and bad characters. Its basic theme is the adventures of a man who has wandered for many years and, when he returns at last to his own country, finds his faithful wife besieged by suitors, whom he kills. When this ancient, wide-spread theme passed into the Trojan cycle, it became a composite epic, attracting and incorporating other equally ancient poetic motifs: its plot has been called the 'despair of all its imitators.'

In its general outline the Odyssey myth is simple:

---

54. This applies to the principal theme, because many of the other parts of the Iliad - hand to hand fighting, standard scenes and descriptions, etc. - belong to the regular traditional epic material.

31

A.   Odysseus, returning to Ithaca from Troy, arrives at Ogygia, the island of the nymph Calypso, who will not allow him to leave. Meanwhile various insolent men, thinking that Odysseus is dead, occupy his palace at Ithaca and seek his wife Penelope in marriage. Then Telemachus, Odysseus' son, on the advice of Athena, visits Nestor at Pylos and Menelaus at Sparta to find out what has become of his father. There he is told that Odysseus is still alive (the first part of the Odyssey, 1-4, is known as the *Telemachy* or Journey of Telemachus).

B.   Hermes comes to Ogygia, sent by the gods on Olympus, and commands Calypso to let Odysseus return to Ithaca. She obeys, but Odysseus' raft is wrecked and he is cast up by the waves on Scheria, the island of the Phaeacians; there Nausicaa, the young daughter of the king of the Phaeacians, Alcinous, finds him and leads him to her father's palace. As a guest of the king, Odysseus reveals who he is and recounts his adventures: how he wandered to the lands of the Ciconians and the Lotus-eaters, to the islands of the Cyclopes, of Aeolus and of Circe, and the country of the Cimmerians; how he escaped the Sirens, and Scylla and Charybdis to reach Thrinacie, the islands where the Sun-god pastures his herds, and how he finally came to Ogygia, Calypso's island, where the goddess held him against his will (the second part, 5-12, is known as the Wanderings of Odysseus).

C.   The Phaeacians entertain Odysseus and afterwards send him on to Ithaca in one of their ships, and there he is received by the swineherd Eumaeus in his hut. But the cautious Odysseus does not tell him immediately who he is. He first waits for his son to recognize him and then, disguised as a beggar, comes to the palace accompanied by Eumaeus. There Argos, his old dog, recognizes his lost master and falls dead on the spot. Various scenes follow, illustrating the insolence of the suitors, and finally Penelope, prompted by Athena, proposes a contest: she promises to marry the one who is strong enough to string Odysseus' bow. Odysseus himself takes part in the contest in spite of the suitors' threats, and is the only one who can handle the great weapon. Aided by Eumaeus, the cowherd Philoetius and his son Telemachus, he kills all the suitors and then punishes all the women slaves who have been unfaithful with death. At last he is recognized by Penelope, but immediately prepares to confront the suitors' allies. Athena, however, intervenes and brings peace to the island of Ithaca (this part,

13-24, is known as the Vengeance of Odysseus).

The structure of the Odyssey is much more complicated than that of the Iliad. We see two threads of narrative, first unwinding separately, and then being joined and closely spun together. In the beginning the epic describes Telemachus' journey in search of his father (1-4); afterwards, when this has come to an end, the narrative begins all over again, in order to describe the Wanderings of Odysseus[55] (5-12). When this narrative in its turn has ended and Odysseus has returned to Ithaca, we turn back to the first thread - that of Telemachus - and see how it is woven in with the second: from now on we have the two stories together of Odysseus and Telemachus, united as they fight side by side against Penelope's suitors and destroy them (15-23). Only then is the hero recognized by his faithful wife Penelope, and the epic reaches its happy close.

When we come to look closely at the text, however, we find, just as in the Iliad, many inconsistencies and difficulties; these caused the Analytical Homerists to expound different theories about the development of the Odyssey, and the use and adaptation in it of earlier lays. Most of these inconsistencies, as well as the abrupt shifts from theme to theme, are caused, in the Odyssey too, by the conflation of different versions of the same episodes and from the additions of later rhapsodes.

The first difficulties begin already in book 1. This book forms an elegant introduction to the whole epic, but it contains one great anomaly in Athena's instructions to Telemachus (269-302), on which the action of the following three books depends. These instructions are not only inconsistent with, but in direct contradiction to lines 88f, and Telemachus ignores them completely.[56] Consequently the Analysts' conclusions seem to be sound, that parts of Athena's speech to Telemachus have been rewritten in a careless, mechanical fashion.[57]

---

55. Telemachus' journey coincides in time with some of Odysseus' wanderings, but epic technique presents synchronous happenings as if they were successive.
56. These proposals of Athena - that Penelope should remarry - would come better from the mouths of the suitors, as in 2. cf Page 1955, 53.
57. A great deal of the Analysts' work is built on the admirable foundations laid down by Kirchoff (1879[2]).

As we proceed, we notice in 2 that in certain places Telemachus' journey is made with the suitors' approval, while in other places it seems clear that the journey is made without it. Probably here as well two variations of the same tale are involved, which have been clumsily joined and interwoven in our Odyssey, and which mutually conflict.[58]

Even the transition from the *Telemachy* to the Wanderings of Odysseus (5, 1f) is not effected in the regular manner. The second assembly of the gods, which takes place at this point, is quite superfluous and takes no account of the previous assembly of the gods (1, 26f) and the decisions taken there by the Olympians.[59]

It has therefore been suggested that these difficulties are due to the composition of the Odyssey; that, in fact, the composer adapted and added to the Wanderings of Odysseus an independent poem about Telemachus' journey. However, although this journey might well once have been an independent work, suitable for separate recital, the combining and blending of Odysseus' wanderings and Telemachus' journey has been accomplished with such deliberateness in books 14-15 (there is no question here of patching or adapting), and the stories of Odysseus and Telemachus in the third part of the Odyssey (13-24) are interwoven in such a complete, organic manner, that we must accept that the same rhapsode shaped both the Telemachy (1-4) and the Vengeance of Odysseus (13-24). And this poet was undoubtedly aided in his work by different earlier lays and themes from Greek epic tradition.

The conflation of earlier sources is also apparent in books 9-12, in which Odysseus tells the Phaeacians of his wanderings. In the two longest accounts - about the land of the Cyclopes (Page 1955, chap. 1; Kirk 1962, 234f) and the visit to Hades - there are clear indications of the

---

58. The clumsy fashion in which the *Telemachy* has been stitched together is also apparent in the awkward transition from Sparta to Ithaca in 4, 620-625. Four comic lines are interpolated at this point, describing a "subscription dinner" with each guest offering a contribution!

59. These are also the only scenes of the gods in the Odyssey. For their structure, etc., v. Page 1955, 70f. The second scene of the gods looks like another independent prologue to the Wanderings of Odysseus (5, 1f), which constitute the most interesting part of the epic and are suitable for separate recital. This scene should not have been included in the complete, monumental Odyssey.

presence of many hands at work. Even in the shorter accounts there are various inconsistencies of composition (Kirk 1962, 234f). Nevertheless, Odysseus' wanderings can be divided into two groups. One comprises the hero's wanderings on the eastern limits of the Greek world, and the other his wanderings which have not been identified geographically or are implied to be in the Western Mediterranean.

Some of these journeys are related to the expedition of the Argonauts (Meuli 1921) and are derived from the earlier Argonaut epics. It should be noted that these stories constitute a nucleus of episodes, at the beginning of which have been added four of Odysseus' wanderings, while their end is linked to his last adventure on Ogygia. But the long episode of the *Nekyia* in 11 has been inserted arbitrarily and is unrelated to the Argonaut expedition. Here the elements of the Descent into Hades have been combined with the more general theme of Necromancy. Probably none of this episode belongs to the original design of the Odyssey, because it presupposes another version of the return of Odysseus. Also many of the differences it displays are due to later additions, the most obvious of which may be seen in lines 568-672.[60] Another addition is the long list of the women who present themselves to Odysseus for no good reason at all [61] (225-330).

However, quite apart from whether it belongs to the original design of the Odyssey or is a later addition, it is to this Homeric Descent into Hades (11) that we owe the 6th book of Virgil's Aeneid and thus, indirectly, all of Dante's Inferno. As others have remarked, what other almost certainly spurious additions to a poem can boast such distinguished progeny?

To the same book (333-384) belongs the strange break in Odysseus' narrative, in order that the poet can describe the hero's conversation with his Phaeacian hosts, which led to his spending one more day in Scheria - while completely ignoring the fact that preparations have already been made for Odysseus' departure that very night, and without giving any

---

60. Aristarchus had already rejected these lines. At this point Odysseus unexpectedly crosses the threshold of Hades and visits the underworld, where he sees Minos, Orion, Tityus, Tantalus and Sisyphus.
61. On the descent into Hades v. Rohde 1895, 600f; Bethe 1929[2], II. 126f Cauer 1921, 363f.; Focke 1943, 177f Page 1955, 21f.

good reason for the postponement.

Inconsistencies are also to be found in the third part of the Odyssey, the Vengeance of Odysseus (13-24). The first inconsistency appears with Odysseus' transformation into an old beggar (13, 397f). The transformation, achieved by supernatural means, disappears in 16 so that Telemachus can recognize his father; later it is repeated so that Odysseus should not be recognized by his servant and the hero now remains transformed until the end. And yet, as the rest of the Odyssey unfolds, it is assumed that such a transformation never took place at all. From the end of 16 onwards, Odysseus is presented as simply changed by the passage of the years and the clothes he has put on.

Another paradoxical element is the role played by Theoclymenus in the Vengeance of Odysseus (13-24). He is given a magnificent introduction (15, 223f) with thirty-two whole lines. It is the lengthiest and most elaborately detailed introduction of its kind in the Odyssey, and this leads us to suppose that Theoclymenus is going to play some important role. And yet his part is very small, confused and absolutely insignificant (Page 1955, 83f). It is therefore probable that this too belongs to some other version of the epic, from which it passed into the Odyssey, having lost its original significance.

Another difficulty arises over the removal of the weapons from the hall in Odysseus' palace. In 16, 281-298 Odysseus and Telemachus agree as to how they are going to strike down the suitors: at a certain moment Odysseus will give a nod and Telemachus will carry all the weapons off to a storeroom (ἐς μυχὸν ὑψηλοῦ θαλάμου), except for two spears, two swords and two shields which they themselves will use in the fight. The first two points of the agreement, however, were not kept, and the third, as it is presented to us, is much changed in the event. It looks therefore as if the original design of book 16 was supplanted by another version. Here too we most probably have two variations of the same episode, which have become jumbled in the Odyssey.

Not even Odysseus' final recognition by Penelope is free from difficulties and inconsistencies. First of all, it is clear from 18, 158-306, that the poet who composed the Slaughter of the Suitors had in his mind another version in which the recognition of Odysseus by Penelope takes place earlier than in the Odyssey. It has therefore been suggested that the recognition in that version must have happened when Penelope finished Laertes' winding-sheet - which coincides with Odysseus arrival at his palace (Kirk 1962, 244f). Nor must we forget that there are two tokens by which he is recognized, the scar (19, 386f and 23, 74f.) and the bed (23, 177f), which is further testimony that two different variations of the myth have been conflated in our Odyssey.

Again, at the end of the Odyssey, the 'Continuation', as it is called (23, 296 to the end of 24), is a transparent later addition. Two of the greatest Alexandrian scholars, Aristophanes of Byzantium and Aristarchus, had already pointed out that the Odyssey ended at 23, 296 (Schol. Od. 23, 296) and that everything which followed was an addition. This has now been accepted by nearly all modern scholars, both Unitarians and Analysts; the linguistic and metrical elements as well as the content itself of this part leave no doubt that it is a more recent composition - probably 6th century BC (Page 1955, 101f).

The inconsistencies we have mentioned are the most conspicuous, but not the only ones to have been observed in the Odyssey (Kirk 1962, 247). To them should be added a certain 'retroverse movement' in the composition of the epic, which also argues against its single-handed creation. Thus, for example, Elpenor's death, at the end of 10, has been devised and modelled on the basis of what the dead Elpenor himself says in 11. And everything that Circe tells Odysseus he must perform in order to gather the dead around him is drawn from what Odysseus himself actually did to achieve precisely that end.

The overall plan of the monumental Odyssey is more complicated than that of the Iliad. The mixing of short episodes with longer, self-contained narratives is less obvious here, while the narration of a large part of the epic by the hero himself marks a great forward step in epic technique. In the Odyssey - for the first time in Western literature - both the flashback and first person narration (Ich-Roman) make their appearance. Hence the passages in which the narrative advances with unbroken continuity and uniformity are much longer in the Odyssey than the Iliad.

It nevertheless remains beyond question that the Odyssey does not exhibit unity of structure, and that it is not the work of one poet. There must have existed at least two earlier versions of the myth about the home-coming, vengeance and recognition of Odysseus, and their elaboration and incorporation into the Odyssey was not carried out faultlessly. The sea adventures also represent a selection from a larger stock of earlier lays, many of which would have been purely folk-tale in character.[62] On the other hand in the *Telemachy* the element of original creation seems to have been considerable, and the episode of the island of the Phaeacians should perhaps be regarded as the most important original contribution of the composer of the Odyssey (Kirk 1962, 363f).

After the monumental epic had been completed, the mechanical incorporation of 'post-Homeric summaries' began; these were perhaps intended to introduce separate recitals of certain episodes, such as the Descent into Hades and the so-called 'Continuation' at the end of the Odyssey.

There are indeed in many places advance disclosures of things to come, just as there are also obvious references to previous events, and comparisons with things that have happened in the past. They all contribute to the articulation of the epic, but reveal nothing of importance about the extent of the later reworking of the original design. Still, it is not hard for us to imagine how a great work of this kind could be expanded, and that undoubtedly happened to the Iliad as much as to the Odyssey.

The unity of the Iliad and the Odyssey is certainly very different from that of a modern literary work, and is no proof that one, and only one poet created each epic. It is on the other hand equally certain that neither of these epics is a random poetic conglomeration around a common heroic theme, or even an anthology of poems about the Trojan war which became casually aligned into some thematic order with the passage of time. Their plots, which are clearly described and which follow an obviously logical order, could equally well be the products of single individuals or of many rhapsodes belonging to one generation, who elaborated a central heroic theme, while naturally making use of much earlier material.

---

62. On this subject v. Carpenter 1946. For the probable Eastern origin of some of these myths with a folktale character, v. Geffcken 1926, I, 41.

In the Odyssey as in the Iliad it appears more likely that the composition of the complicated material into a monumental epic was the work of one man (v. 28f), but took place in the 7th century. In other words, the Odyssey is later than the Iliad and, in a certain way, a rival of the older great epic. Insofar as the composer of the monumental Odyssey is assigned to the 7th century, he cannot have been Homer, who, as we have seen, must have lived earlier. Nor can we isolate the part Homer may have played in the composition of the Odyssey - assuming that he had any part in it at all. Homer, who probably lived in the 8th century, may very well have had an Odyssey in his repertoire, but it was certainly not the same as the Odyssey we have in our hands today. Once again the *ipsissima verba* of the great poet must remain beyond our grasp. It is in any case certain that both great epics originated in Ionia; so much is apparent from the linguistic and other evidence. In the case of the Odyssey we have the added indication that nothing in it bears witness to a knowledge of the main Helladic world, just as nowhere is a direct acquaintance with Ithaca apparent.[63]

Finally we should add that all the geography in the Odyssey is poetical and not real. Even in Hellenistic times Eratosthenes rightly rejected and derided all attempts to trace Odysseus' wanderings on the map. Many in our own time have embarked with persistence on this vain pursuit. It is obvious, however, that Odysseus is straying in the lands of myth, beyond the bounds of the world known to men. The details of his wanderings never existed outside the poet's imagination.

The Odyssey taken as a whole is a wonderful achievement and contains some of the most splendid poetical descriptions of all time - such as Odysseus' being cast up on Scheria and his meeting with Nausicaa (14, 41f), the little islet across from the island of the Cyclopes (9, 116f), Odysseus' arrival at Ithaca (13, 78f), the episode with Odysseus' dog, Argos (17, 290f) or the morning bustle in the palace (20, 147f). Along with these there are such striking touches of irony, tenderness, imagination, subtle lyricism, fantasy and nobility of spirit, competing with - and

---

63. If Ithaca is present day Thiaki, then the poet of the Odyssey is mistaken about its position (9, 25), its fertility (13, 244; 19, 399), and the island of Asteris (4, 846). This led Doerpfeld (1927) to suggest that the Homeric Ithaca was present day Lefkas. The description undoubtedly matches Lefkas better, but the change of name is inexplicable.

in some cases surpassing - similar scenes in the Iliad. And yet the Odyssey never really achieves either the depth or the greatness of the Iliad. This is largely due to its theme, which is at once less catholic and less tragic. [64] It is also due in some measure to the character of the central hero, Odysseus, who, while heroic, alert and versatile, has not the magnificence of god-like Achilles. To a considerable degree this is also the result of the style of the Odyssey, which is flatter than that of the Iliad. During many long drawn-out passages interest wanes because the narrative is excessively protracted (sometimes one has the impression that it is simply trying to compete with the Iliad in length), and because the language is smoother and less lively than in the Iliad.

Furthermore, the similes and the scenes with gods - which vary and enliven epic narrative - are much rarer in the Odyssey than in the Iliad, while scenes of everyday life - such as conventional descriptions of the preparation of food, of sacrifices, arrivals, departures etc. - are commoner; and there are many long digressions which interrupt the narrative (eg 14, 457f). Moreover many longer passages of the Odyssey are repeated in other parts of the text in a more condensed form. [65]

Hence the Odyssey lacks the liveliness and tautness which characterize even the lesser episodes in the Iliad. It must not be forgotten, however, that all these flaws we have detailed only become noticeable when we compare it with the supreme achievement of the Iliad. By any other standard the Odyssey is, as it has properly been considered for two and a half thousand years, one of the greatest triumphs of human genius.

---

64. In the final analysis the plot of the Odyssey consists in the evolution of a moral and religious concept - that of rewarding good and punishing evil.
65. eg lines 17, 427-441 are part of a longer account in 14. Lines 12, 403-425 are summed up in 14, 301f, etc. .

CHAPTER THREE – THE DATE OF THE HOMERIC EPICS AND THEIR FORM.

The Homeric hexameter.

The metre of the Homeric epics is the dactylic hexameter:

$$- \overline{uu} \; / \; - \overline{uu} \; / \; - \overline{uu} \; / \; - \overline{uu} \; / \; - \overline{uu} \; / \; - \underline{u}$$

Like all ancient metres it is quantitative, in the sense that the metric value of the syllable is determined by its quantity, in other words its length, and not by the accent, the sounded stress. In the Homeric hexameter the rule also obtains whereby the dactyl (−uu) can be replaced by a spondee (− −) provided that the exchange does not occur at the same place in every line. This possibility, together with the division of the line into two parts[1] by a caesura, allowed the poet a remarkable variety of rhythms without losing the basic dactylic rhythm of the line.

Nothing certain is known about the origin of the dactylic hexameter. The hypothesis has been put forward - without any proof - that its origin is Minoan or Hittite and not Mycenean. It has even been contended that it grew out of a combination of two or more earlier meters, but there is no evidence for this either. What is certain, however, is that originally the hexameter was not recited but sung; in the Homeric epics Achilles, Demodocus and Phemius sing the "tidings of men" accompanied by the *phorminx,* the lyre (IX, 186f; 8, 261; 22, 332). And the poet himself, be it noted, calls on the muse to "sing": "Sing of the wrath, O Goddess, of Peleus' son, Achilles . . . " (I, 1). It was probably some kind of simple, 'primitive' song without a proper melody. For in its composition heroic poetry exclusively employed as a unit the dactylic line, which was sung or recited by a single bard or rhapsodist; it made no use of composite metres like those developed later in lyric poetry.

---

1. There are three such *caesurae* in Homeric poetry: 1) after the first syllable of the third foot (the so-called masculine caesura) 2) after the second syllable of the third foot, provided that it is a dactyl (the so-called feminine caesura) and 3) after the first syllable of the fourth foot.

41

It may also be observed that the Greek language lends itself more naturally and easily to iambic triameters than to hexameters (cf Aristotle, *Poetics,* 1449a 25). If however in the Mycenean period, when the hexameter began to come into use, the Greek language had more uncontracted forms than we find in it later on, then the work of the heroic poet would have been easier. In any case, epic poetry shows how, by artificially lengthening a short syllable - in other words, quickening the prosody - it was able to use various intractable words in the line.

The hexameter is a remarkable narrative metre, the like of which is not found in any other part of the world, and which contributes to preserving the musicality and liveliness of the language. The skill with which the Greek epic poets of the oral tradition combined the complex technique of the hexameter with their direct narrative manner is really extraordinary. (Bowra 1962, 19; Wilamowitz-Moellendorff 1920, 352; Witte 1913; Schulze 1892).

The language of the Homeric epics: a linguistic amalgam.

Many of the forms in the manuscripts of the Homeric epics are undoubtedly orthographic errors which crept in when the text was first written down (Palmer 1968, 17f; Wace and Stubbings 1962, 75-178). But even when these errors have been corrected, the Homeric language still exhibits a strange mixture. It is basically an Ionic dialect (η generally replacing a), but containing Aeolic elements.[2] Along with these there are some minor Attic elements (Wackernagel 1916), which show that the Homeric epics were already 'finished' when they came to Athens, and that very few changes took place there.

Various theories have been put forward to explain this mixture of dialects,[3] but none has been generally accepted. The inescapable conclusion is that this linguistic alloy is a characteristic element in the language which was used for the composition of the Homeric epics right from the

---

2.   v. Chantraine 1957; Schwyzer 1939 I, 106f. The question of aeolisms became the subject of renewed debate after the decipherment of the Linear B tablets, without however any agreement being reached. v. Platnauer 1968, 43f.
3.   v. Fick 1883; 1886; Bechtel 1901; 1908; Wilamowitz-Moellendorff 1906, 61f; Ruijgh 1957.

beginning.[4] In spite of much recent discussion about this question,[5] the generally prevalent view of the epic language has not changed: G. S. Kirk sums it up well when he writes that "the Iliad and Odyssey are the culmination of a continuous tradition of oral poetry", and that "their linguistic components are of diverse origin both in locality and date." (1962, 192). If this is true it is extraordinary and hardly explicable that poetry of such greatness and liveliness should have employed an artificial language that was never spoken, and which, therefore, its poet-creators never knew as a mother tongue. It is equally extraordinary that Greek poetry should have admired and imitated this 'artificial' poetic idiom for over a millenium and a half.

The technique of the formulas.

Homeric narrative depends to a large degree on the structure of the dactylic hexameter. The poets, in order to create a language that was adapted to the needs of versification, and at the same time capable of ensuring against any break in the narration, fashioned a series of stock phrases, each with its fixed position in the line, which we call 'formulas'. The most usual of these stock phrases - those referring to various common ideas and situations[6] - fill the space between the bucolic diaeresis, or one of the three Homeric caesuras, and the end of the line. Other such phrases fill the space between the beginning of the line and the hexameter caesuras. Others, again, occupy a whole line or series of lines. Certain categories of descriptions belong to these stock phrases - the preparation of food or of a sacrifice, the departure of a ship, the reception of a guest, etc - , many of which occupy a number of lines and are repeated in various similar situations.[7] And we must not forget that Greek epic

---

4. The view that the epic language was artificial was also held by Witte (1913, 2213f) and Meister (1921). The fact that the digamma is not employed consistently is still another indication that the epic language is in fact an artificial one. v. Chantraine 1942 I, 116f.

5. For the so-called Porzig-Risch theory v. Chadwick 1956; Chadwick 1963. It maintains that the West Greek and Aeolic dialects should be regarded as the offspring of a North Mycenean language and that the Arcado-Cypriote, and Attic-Ionic are descended from a South Mycenean. For the repercussions of this theory on the question of poetic language v. Platnauer 1968, 44f; Kirk 1964, 90f.

6. Parallel formulas for the same thing are very rare.

7. There are word for word repetitions not only of stock phrases and descriptions

poetry is formular both in subject matter and language; this is true not only of the major themes which, as we have seen, form the broad structure of the epic, but of many minor ones as well, which are woven into the narrative.

Among the chief formulaic elements is the use of the ornamental epithet that always accompanies the same noun. Such constant characterizations exist for gods and heroes, things and places, situations and actions, and so on.[8] This repeated and unvarying usage ends by diluting the original descriptive power of the ornamental epithet, so that gradually the epithet comes to characterize the epic style in general and no longer the particular noun which it accompanies. This is also the reason that certain ornamental epithets are inappropriate to the sense of the context. The sky, for example, is described as 'starry' even during the day; ships are called 'swift' even when they are at anchor; the swineherd in the Odyssey is described as 'noble' and the mother of the beggar Irus as 'revered'. It is remarkable how few Homeric epithets are applied to more than one noun. But when nearly everything that is presented is accompanied by one constant epithet, the style acquires a certain ceremonial formality. In this way the stock epithets applied to a hero, a cup, a shield or a ship make these things more estimable, and lend an additional touch of formality, a dignity to the narrative style.

Although this free use of so many stereotyped components strikes us as unfamiliar, we soon learn that the choice of each stock phrase has been made with as much care as the choice of words in written poetry. The phrasal unit of epic poetry is not the word, but the formula, the phrase; the poet adapts the ready-made phrases so that they fit into the flow of his verses. The older stock phrases are naturally also combined with new phrases (or lines), thus extending further the material that has already become standardized. The work of the maker of oral poetry is by no means performed mechanically, nor is it lacking in originality.

The product of this process has an astonishing vitality. Equally, too, the skill with which the traditional phraseology is manipulated is not one

---

of certain scenes, but also of many messages (eg XI, 187-194 = XI, 200-210; XV, 160-167 = XV, 176-183, etc.); this is a common characteristic of oral poetry.

8. On Homeric ornamental epithets v. Düntzer 1872, 508; Parry 1928; 1930, 73f.

wit less astonishing than the Homeric literary language itself which, as we have seen, was never spoken in any part of the Greek world.

Two more important elements of Homeric style are due to the technique of stock phrases. The first is the survival of archaic words whose meaning had already been forgotten - the great scholars of antiquity themselves often did not know their meaning (Leumann 1950) - and so these words became purely ornamental elements having only a vague suggestiveness and a beautiful sound. The second is that the formulaic technique is also responsible for the social and political blend we find in the epics; this has given us many extraordinary composite descriptions of things which never existed as they are described and do not correspond to any reality (v. 65f)

The diversity of style.

Epic poetry exhibits a marked diversity of style, and this gives life to the narrative.

Generally we find a smooth, periodic style in both the Iliad and the Odyssey, although it is flatter in the latter.[9] Alongside this in many places we find a compact narrative style which occasionally gives a certain impression of obscurity.[10]

As opposed to these two manners, at certain dramatic and formal moments the language becomes stately and sonorous. We then have a style that may be described as 'majestic', which is in direct contrast to the usual simple flow of Homeric narrative. Examples of this style are found in Zeus' oath to Thetis (I, 528-530), and the description of Athena (V, 733-747). The stateliness of the language is enhanced by the use of long, sonorous words and of hyperbole. The majestic style, which is not found in the Odyssey, is rare also in the Iliad; it is often not found even in those parts of the epic where it would heighten the drama.

9. On the Homeric 'paratactic' style v. Chantraine 1942 II, 351f.
10. eg in lines IX, 550f or XVII, 605f. This interweaving of themes and phrases is the result of the paratactic nature of Homeric poetry, in other words of the fact that thoughts which are logically dependent are presented as separate, grammatically coordinated propositions. The effect of this tendency is to produce occasionally a terse style which resorts to generalizations or to an exaggerated concentration of detail.

Akin to the majestic style is the 'ornamental lyric style', which is employed particularly for the descriptions of gods, and which is not found in the Odyssey in its more extreme form. It is largely limited to the long episode known as the Beguilement of Zeus, which occupies a large part of books XIII-XV. Typical examples of this style are to be found in the lines XIII, 18f and XIV, 347-351; they are in a way reminiscent of Aeolic lyric poetry, which followed the epic.

There are, naturally, countless lyric passages in the Iliad and Odyssey, but their lyricism does not extend beyond an epithet or a single phrase, and so cannot be said to constitute a proper style. For the same reason the occasional use of stress and variation (which depends on a careful arrangement of words and phrases) cannot be called the 'rhetorical' style in the epics.[11]

Thus the two Homeric epics display both unity and diversity of style,[12] indispensable qualities in such long poems. The Odyssey, significantly, has less diversity of style, and the use of hyperbole is mainly confined to certain long expansions, such as the Continuation (23, 295 to end of 24).

The cultural amalgam.

The Homeric epics present a cultural as well as linguistic amalgam, and this is due largely to the formulas and the stereotyped character of Greek epic poetry.

There is undoubted evidence that many elements in the Homeric epics relate to the Mycenean period, and that various descriptions (in spite of the later additions and amendments that are detectable in certain instances) correspond to archaeological finds of the Mycenean period. Some of these descriptions, indeed, like the body-shield or

---

11. To which belong, for example, the poet's rhetorical questions (V, 703; 3, 113f), the way in which he invokes divine inspiration (I, 1f; 1, 1f) or his dramatic apostrophes to one of the heroes (XVI, 787; 14, 165), the emphatic repetition of words and phrases (I, 266f; XX, 371f), the use of assonance and alliteration (I, 49f; V, 440), as well as the use of antithesis (VII, 93) and the methodical juxtaposition of a series of words (11, 612).
12. This diversity is partly due also to the origins of the two poems as oral poetry.

Nestor's cup, belong to the early part of the period, that of the shaft-graves found in the acropolis of Mycenae (ca. 1600 BC).

Thus certain epithets, objects and incidents characteristic of the Mycenean civilization do go back to the Mycenean period, such as the body-shield, the silver-studded sword, Nestor's cup, the *zoma* we find in Odyssey ·14, 482, the abundance of precious metals, the technique of metal inlay, the bronze weapons and tools, the use of the single thrust-ing-spear, the boar's-tusk helmet, and the helmets with horns (*phaloi*) and crests (*lophoi*) (Gray 1968, 28f. 46f). The absence of Dorians from the epics must also be attributed to that period, as well as the Mycenean opulence and their sovereignty over all the Greek world, the general political organization of the Iliad (Nilsson 1933, 212f), and a part of the Catalogue of Ships (book II).

Equally, however, other elements relate to the Geometric and the beginning of the Orientalizing periods. Among the Geometric period elements for example, are the cremation of the dead,[13] the pair of light casting-spears, the leather shields with bronze sheathing and no blazons, the axes, knives and arrow-heads of iron; and similarly the knowledge of iron-working (which is obvious in the similes and metaphors), the womens' clothing, the illiteracy and the references to Phoenician trading in the Aegean, something that would have been impossible as long as the Myceneans dominated Greek seas. These numerous elements show that the composition of a large part of the epics must have taken place in the post-Mycenean period.

On the other hand there are very few elements from post-Geometric times, and perhaps even these are not integrated organically in the epics. Such elements are Athena's lamp and Odysseus' brooch in the Odyssey, or the references to the hoplite armament and tactics[14], and the Gorgon-head as a decorative motif, in the Iliad (Hampe 1936, 63).

---

13.   There are some instances of cremation in the 12th century, but in regular cemeteries where the dead were buried; cf Desborough 1967, 71.

14.   It is now thought that the development of the phalanx came about gradually and was not a sudden revolution in the art of warfare occurring around 700 BC; v. Snodgrass 1964, 138.

The cultural amalgam does not end with the post-Geometric period. There are also elements belonging to the 6th and 5th centuries BC which should not be overlooked. The most important are Nestor's speech in VII, 334f of the Iliad (cf Jacoby 1944, 37f); lines II, 192-197, which were unknown to Xenophon and had already been athetized by Aristarchus; lines II, 853-855, which were not in the text considered genuine by Apollodorus, but would have been added in the 3rd or 2nd century BC (cf Page 1959, 315f. 340).

These elements, however, belonging to such different periods, cannot be used to distinguish a stratification of the narratives, nor help to date that part of the epic where they occur. The description of Hector's shield, for example, comes in VI, that of Nestor's cup in IX, and that of Hector's spear in VI and VII, and all these books are with reason considered 'late' in the history of the Iliad. Finally, the boar's tusk helmet occurs in X, which is certainly the latest major addition to the Iliad.[15]

In this way elements of the Mycenean and Orientalizing periods - ignoring the few much later elements - separated in time by more than a millenium, became fused into an inseparable alloy. This alloy is the product of the epic technique of formulas, of stock phrases, as a result of which the earlier elements continued to be used and incorporated into later narrative strata. Literary analysis, therefore, cannot separate out this extraordinary blend beyond a certain, limited degree.

Hence epic narrative has been compared with a dough, in which different elements have been gradually kneaded, but which can no longer be separated into earlier and later parts, even though certain of these ingredients can be isolated and, once isolated, dated individually. It should, however, be noted that the Mycenean components occur chiefly as essential elements in the story or in formulaic passages, but rarely in the short descriptive scenes; moreover in the Odyssey they are far fewer than in the Iliad, although certain parts of the Odyssey are as early as the earliest parts of the Iliad. On the other hand the Geometric elements,

---

15. The composition of book X apparently took place after the Odyssey, because it depicts Odysseus armed with a bow, whereas everywhere else in the Iliad he is armed with spear and sword. Odysseus' bow in X undoubtedly has its origin in the bow which played such an important part in the conclusion of the Odyssey.

which are extensive, manifest themselves for the most part in the manner in which the poet narrates different scenes, or in the similes he uses.

Nevertheless, for all that the world of the epics is such a curious amalgam, it manages to create the illusion that it is a real world, and that it once actually did exist with all its suffering and all its glory.

Differences between the Iliad and the Odyssey.

No one will dispute that there are very obvious differences between the Iliad and the Odyssey, and that the differences do not consist only in the more 'realistic' spirit of the one and the more 'romantic' character of the other. Nor are the differences just a matter of poetic tension, which is much slacker in the Odyssey - a difference that was beautifully expressed by Pseudo-Longinus (who in fact believed Homer to have been the poet of both epics): "In the Odyssey Homer may be compared to the setting sun; he retains all his magnitude but not his power" ('Longinus' IX, 13).

1.   The first important difference is to be found in the vocabulary of the Odyssey, which diverges from that of the Iliad more than the differences in the subject matter require (cf Page 1959, 149f), and in which the disappearance or the diminished use of old words is accompanied by the appearance of relatively new ones.[16] This can be observed in the use of words, and in the stock phrases, many of which now appear in a debased manner in the Odyssey.[17]

In general the linguistic differences are such that it has even been suggested that the Iliad and the Odyssey belong to two different branches of the epic tradition, even though in the final analysis they have a common stem (Page 1959, 149f; Monro 1901 II, 325). This view receives further support from the fact that the Odyssey completely ignores the

16.   On the one hand obselete epithets, Σμινθεύς, βοῶπις, ἐκηβόλος, etc., are absent from the Odyssey, and on the other neologisms, like οὕνεκα, (= that), πρῆξις (business), χρήματα and new abstract nouns like ὁσίη or εὐνομίη, make their appearance in it.
17.   eg the "πίονα πενταέτηρον" in 14, 419 for the swine (in Iliad II, 403 the stock phrase is used correctly for the ox and not for the swine); or the phrase "ἤριπε δὲ πρηνής" in 22, 296 for somebody who receives a blow from the front.

Iliad; it makes no mention of any of the episodes in the Iliad, although it harks back in places to some of the events of the Trojan War (eg 4, 235f; 4, 266f; 5, 309f; 8, 74f; 11, 543f).

2.   The second striking difference lies in the morality of the two epics and the manner in which the gods are presented. In the Odyssey, unlike the Iliad, the gods are concerned with the moral aspect of human actions (Reinhardt 1950). When, in the first scene of the gods (1, 1f), Zeus censures humans who attribute all their troubles to the gods, he is at the same time proclaiming that mortals themselves are responsible for the ills that beset them. In general the whole of the Odyssey, as we have seen, is a moral lesson - of the rewarding of good and punishing of evil - and is different from the dark, tragic Iliad, where everything in the end is destroyed.

There is nothing in the Iliad comparable to 23,67 (cf 24, 351), where we learn that the suitors have been punished for their 'wicked ways'. It is clear that the Odyssey is inspired by a more 'moral' spirit than the Iliad, and this may be because by the 7th century the idea had already developed that the gods took an interest in the morality of human actions.

Not only the gods, but humans have greater moral feelings in the Odyssey. After the slaughter of the suitors Eurycleia utters a shout of triumph, but Odysseus scolds her, telling her that it is wrong to exult over the dead (22, 412). What a striking contrast to Achilles' attitude after he has killed Hector in Iliad XXII!

3.   We find a third important difference in the social organization in the two epics; in the Odyssey it has advanced to the point where the institution of kingship is beginning to disintegrate and the aristocratic clans are becoming dominant. While in the Iliad we are given a picture of a closed, exclusive noble class, in the Odyssey the social framework is much broader. Here the epic has opened the doors to the wants and ideas of social classes which were unknown in the Iliad (Jacoby 1933, 159; Finley 1956) and this gives the Odyssey a later, more modern tone.

4.   A fourth important point is that in the Odyssey the Mycenean elements - although they occur in both epics - are much fewer. This

means that the composition of the Odyssey is later than that of the Iliad. This later date is also suggested by Odysseus' interest in nautical adventures - which reflect the beginning of the era of great sea voyages and explorations - and is something entirely different from the attitudes and ideals of the heroes who fought before the walls of Troy. Basically the Odyssey is more an adventure novel than a real epic - it is a story with a happy ending, with both good and bad characters, and closer to folk tale than saga. This illustrates the change in social ideas that took place between the time when the Iliad was acquiring its monumental form and the time when the Odyssey acquired its final form.

The Odyssey also marks a great step forward in the technique of composing monumental works. In the Iliad there are many independent passages and episodes which could be excised without destroying the whole, [18] while the plot of the Odyssey is so tightly knit that, if we except Telemachus' Journey (1-4), very few parts can be considered entirely independent, self-contained episodes.

5.   A fifth difference is noticeable in the mythological modernisms of the Odyssey. There Hermes is the messenger of the Gods, while in the Iliad Iris plays this role; Hephaestus is Aphrodite's husband (8, 268), while in the Iliad he is Charis' husband (XVIII, 382); the Dioscuri enjoy divine immortality (11, 300), while in the Iliad they are common mortals (III, 237-244). In the Odyssey, again, there are certain private beliefs or superstitions not known in the Iliad.[19]

6.   A sixth difference to be noted is the use of the bow. In the Odyssey it plays the principal role in the epic's conclusion (8, 215); in the Iliad, on the other hand, it is not an important weapon, and the great heroes do not deign to use it. Only in the *Doloneia* (X) does Odysseus handle one - and then, indeed, uses it to whip his horse; but all of this book is later and probably acquired its present form after the Odyssey (v. 396 n. 16).

------

18. Like the Catalogue of Ships in II, the exploits of Diomedes in V, of Agamemnon in XI, or the ransoming of Hector's body in XXIV.
19. Thus we have Circe making magic, Teiresias instructing Odysseus on how to summon the dead (in 11), and we also have evil daemons (5, 396; 10, 64; 24, 14), dogs with second sight (16, 161f), sneezing as an omen (17, 541f), and the power of kings to influence crops and fertility (19, 111).

7.   Another noteworthy element is the advance shown by the Odyssey in the description of 'town-scenes' and of women. This is of course partly due to the subject matter itself, which calls for such descriptions. At the same time, however, these scenes also reflect the new topics of interest which were finding their way into epic poetry at that time. Such are the descriptions of the palaces of Menelaus at Sparta, of Alcinous on Scheria or of Odysseus on Ithaca, which are in all probability composite and do not correspond to actual palaces, but were more likely to satisfy the popular demand to hear about such marvellous edifices.

What is particularly impressive in the Odyssey, however, is the way in which women are portrayed; the range of female types is impressive and so is the very real understanding exhibited of their psychology.[20] Thus we have Calypso, woman as well as goddess, revealing a strongly sentimental side, and next to her the noble, maidenly purity of Nausicaa; and then Penelope with her wifely dignity and fidelity, and beside her a real old shrew, Eurycleia. It is a sign that women were gaining ground in the Ionian world at the time when epic poetry had already started to decline.[21]

All these major differences, as well as other lesser ones, show that the Iliad and Odyssey were not both the works of the same poet. Further-more neither of them individually, as we have said, was the work of a single man. We can only accept that they were the fruit of the work of many talented poets belonging to different generations, even if, in one form or other, they might both have formed a part of the repertoire of Homer - that great unknown figure in the history of Greek poetry.

The dating of the 'monumental' compositions and the basic stages in their transmission.

Having considered the forms and the remarkable cultural amalgam of the Homeric epics, and having noted the basic differences between

---

20.   The only scene in the Iliad where feminine psychology is given a full description is the farewell between Hector and Andromache in VI, and this is thought to be 'late'.
21.   There is no reason to insist here on the difference between the intrepid Achilles of the Iliad and the Achilles who displays such a love for life in Odyssey 11. A spirit living in Hades is bound to be different from a live hero.

them, we can now turn back to the problem of their chronology and to the decisive stages in their transmission down to the present day.

Literally speaking, of course, one cannot speak of 'dating' works belonging to an oral tradition that lasted for centuries; for as we have seen, the themes, formulas, conventional descriptions, and so on, have their roots in different historical periods, and have been reworked and reshaped by successive generations of rhapsodes.

In spite of this, it is not impossible to date the monumental Homeric compositions in a general way, or in other words, to fix the time when the Iliad and Odyssey had already been 'finished'.

In this difficult task we are assisted first of all by certain dateable elements which are found in the epics themselves, and secondly, by certain dateable external effects of the poems we can lay our hands on.

1) Archaeological and linguistic criteria date certain elements in the epics. It is sure, for example, that they contain nothing which, by archaeological criteria, can be dated after 700 BC, with the sole exception of the Attic custom of bringing back the ashes of warriors killed in distant campaigns to be buried in their own country [22] (VII, 334f). On the other hand there are certain elements, such as the references to the Phoenicians, the two light casting-spears used in battle, and perhaps the separate, roofed temples,[23] which are not earlier than about 900 BC. There are also only few and isolated elements which can be attributed to the 8th rather than the 9th century, such as the appearance of hoplite tactics,[24] or the gorgon-head used as a decorative motif. Indeed, the gorgon-head on Agamemnon's shield may well be a later addition, a two-line amendment introduced into the Iliad to cater for a generation which had already started to embellish its shields with blazons.[25]

---

22. A 5th century Attic practice; v. Jacoby 1944, 37f; Page 1959, 315f.
23. But v. Caskey 1966, 367f.
24. Hoplites make a gradual appearance in the Greek world, and the introduction of the phalanx does not bring about a revolution in military tactics at c. 700 BC, as used to be thought; v. Snodgrass 1964, 138.
25. Athena's lamp and Odysseus' pin in the Odyssey are much too vague to warrant more general conclusions. The same applies to the comparison between Homeric shields and cups and those from Crete and Phoenicia; v. Kirk 1962, 282f; Gray 1968, 29.

The linguistic criteria, it must be admitted, unfortunately do not help us much to date the epics more closely. The epic style - including both the use of formulas and metrical variations, such as the frequency with which the bucolic diaeresis appears - shows that the Iliad and Odyssey are earlier then Hesiod (ca.680 BC ?) and the oldest of the Homeric Hymns (ca.650 BC); just how much older the epics are, cannot be settled with any exactness. Even certain later elements that appear in the mixed Homeric language - such as the use of the demonstrative pronoun with the full meaning of the definite article or the formation of verbal abstracts - do not preclude dating the epics to around the 9th or 8th century.

2)   The external elements that help to date the epics consist of certain direct quotations from the Homeric epics,[26] as well as indirect references to them, found in other poets. In the elegaic, lyric and iambic poetry of the 7th century, especially Archilochus, Alcman, Callinus and Tyrtaeus, we find many epithets, formulas and half-lines taken from epic poetry. To these may be added the lines found written on a vase from Ischia, referring to Nestor's famous cup (XI, 632f), and the Ischia vase is dated before 700 BC (Kirk 1962, 70; Gray 1968, 48)

Then there are the epic scenes depicted on vases, which show that the 8th and 7th centuries were interested in the epic myths (Gray 1962, 48). But the oldest certain representations of epic scenes are dated to after 700, and later than the Geometric vases belonging to the period 675-650 BC[27] (Kirk 1962, 285).

Finally we should mention the appearance of hero cults in the Greek world, which is dated from the 8th century (Cook 1953, 30f), because one of its causes is thought to be the dissemination of the Homeric epics through mainland Greece.

All these factors are not sufficient, of course, to date the 'monumental' composition of the two epics with any precision. And naturally we cannot call on the testimony of the ancient sources for Homer's

26.   Some of these probably belong to the general stock of epic poetry and have no direct connection with the Iliad and Odyssey.
27.   v. Kirk, 1962, 285. Most of these themes are taken from other epics of the epic cycle and not from the Iliad and the Odyssey.

chronology (v. 1f), since we do not know what part he played in shaping them.

What we must not forget, however, is that in the middle of the 7th century personal poetry made its appearance with the elegiac, iambic and lyric poets. This implies that the old impersonal rhapsodes, like those who composed the Iliad and Odyssey, already belonged to the past. For this reason it can be convincingly argued that the epic tradition survived and was actively creative until about 700 BC; thereafter any actual innovatory process ceased.[28]

We can say in conclusion that according to the evidence available the Iliad and Odyssey acquired their finished form by the 9th or 8th century; and that a number of factors argue in favour of the 8th century, such as the appearance of representations of the Trojan Cycle on vases, the hero-cults and the reference to hoplites. These all suggest ca. 750 BC as a *terminus post quem*.

Hence it is that, in a general way and very tentatively, the date of the 'monumental' Iliad can be set in the 8th century. Since, as the similarity of styles indicates, the probable date of the 'monumental' Odyssey should not be more than two or three generations later than the Iliad, it may be placed at the end of the 8th or beginning of the 7th century.

Our ignorance of the events of the 9th and 8th, and the first half of the 7th centuries is so great that we cannot expect to locate the dates of the monumental Homeric compositions with any more precision.

The principal stages in the transmission of the epics.

If the Homeric epics were composed without the use of writing, then the question of when they were written down is of major importance. As we saw when we examined the structure of the Iliad, we are not in a position to say whether the poet (or poets) of the monumental epics were the same ones who first wrote them down in the 8th and 7th centuries, or whether they - or later poets - dictated them to some other persons.

---

28. On the theory of the 'creative' and 'reproductive' stages in the epic tradition, v. Kirk 1962, 95f.

It has been justifiably argued that no poet or public would have any reason to want to have the poems written down in a society where oral poetry was still flourishing - unless they were stimulated to do so by some special circumstance or motive. [29] Many scholars have considered that this circumstance arose with the celebration of the Panathenaea in the 6th century (Cauer 1921; Wackernagel 1916), when the Homeric epics were recited from a cue (ἐξ ὑποβολῆς) and each rhapsode took up at the point where the one before left off. [30]

When, however, we consider the wide diffusion of the Homeric epics in Ionia, the islands and mainland Greece in the 7th century, as well as the fact that by then oral poetry had already started to decline, the opinion that the Iliad and Odyssey were first committed to writing in Athens seems unlikely. Besides, as we have seen above, there are no significant 7th or 6th century interpolations in the text which has come down to us.

However, even if the version that was produced in Athens was not the first written text of the Homeric epics, the report of a 6th century Attic Homeric text must have some truth in it.

This is attested first of all by the dispute which broke out in the 4th century between the Athenians and the Megarians over the charge that interpolations had been inserted into the Homeric epics. During this dispute it is clear that both sides believed a written version of the Homeric epics had been made in Athens in the 6th century. And secondly it would appear from this dispute that no other redactions were in circulation in mainland Greece at that time, with which comparisons

---

29. v. Carpenter 1946, 14. On the technical facilities for writing down the epics v. Bethe 1946, 16. 110.

30. The reports about the 'Athenian' recension of the epics are confused. Some ancient authorities attribute it to Peisistratus (Cic. *de Oratore* III, 34, 137; Paus. VII 26; Anth. Pal. XI 442), others to Solon (Diog. Laertes I 2.9) and one source to Hipparchus (Pseudo-Plato, *Hipparchus* 228 B; cf also Lycurgus, *Contra Leocr.* 102). Some reports tell us further that a commission was set up of seventy-two members (including Zenodotus and Aristarchus), and others, a commission of four members (including Orpheus!), in order to produce an edition of the Homeric epics. The name of Onomacritus is associated with these commissions; (cf. Herod. VII 6). v. Mazon 1967, 271; Davison 1962, 215f; Allen 1924, 230.

could be made. Moreover a study of Homer's language and, especially of its spelling, as we find it in our manuscripts, shows clearly that the manuscripts which have reached us are the descendants of an original Athenian draft.[31]

A written version, then, which was made early on and in Athens, may be taken as one of the principal stages in the transmission of the Homeric epics, even if we cannot prove that it happened also to have been the first written text.

This Athenian text seems to have been copied from then on, and to have circulated more or less as a standard version of the two epics, and the paramount position it acquired in the Greek world is undoubtedly due to the political, cultural and commercial importance of 5th century Athens. This fact must have contributed to the disappearance of other known editions of Homer, because the Alexandrian scholars inform us that three other sorts of Homeric texts had existed. These were: the 'city editions' (*kata poleis*), that is editions put out in different cities; 'private' (*kat' andra*) editions, those made by private individuals; and the 'multi-verse' edition (*polystichos*), which contained more lines than any of the others and was in other words an enlarged edition of Homer.[32] None of these seems to have influenced significantly the vulgate which has come down to us. Even the oral transmission of the text, which seems to have survived on into the 6th century, does not appear to have added anything to it except for a few minor variations of the verses in the 'official' Attic edition.

Consequently the editing of the Homeric text in the Alexandrian period was carried out on one or more of the manuscript descendants of the Athenian edition, and it was on these that Zenodotus (who flourished around 290 BC), Aristophanes of Byzantium (around 220 BC), and especially Aristarchus (217-145 BC) worked[33] (Pfeiffer 1968, 105f. 171f. 210f). Aristarchus' revised edition subsequently became the standard text for all later generations. Innumerable fragments of Homeric

31. The central fact is certain even though various details about its geneology are conjectural. v. Palmer 1968, 17f. 42f.
32. The Homeric Scholia tell us about the editions of Chios, Marseilles, Argos, Cyprus and Crete; v. Mazon 1948, 24. 67.
33. The *editio princeps* of Homer was made by Demetrius Chalcocondyles in 1488.

papyri from the 1st century AD onwards (for half a millenium) show that the Homer we have today is the one edited by Aristarchus, a direct descendant of his 'standard' text, and that since then no significant changes in the Homeric text have occurred. This, the last important stage in the transmission of the Homeric epics, was the Alexandrian, and it is dated between the 3rd and 2nd centuries BC.

CHAPTER FOUR — EPIC NARRATIVE TECHNIQUE

The three manners of epic narrative.

In the Homeric epics three poetic narrative manners can be distinguished: 1) the objective, where the poet himself is not present and the myth proceeds as if it were unfolding on its own; 2) the subjective, where the poet intervenes directly in order to interpret or clarify certain aspects of the action; and 3) the dramatic, where the heroes themselves develop the plot or reveal their own personalities by direct speech. The third manner is used much more than the other two, and is commoner in the Odyssey than in the Iliad.[1]

The chief characteristics of the objective manner are the directness and simplicity of the narrative. These two features are undoubtedly the result of the oral transmission of the epics, which required that special attention be paid to the audience.[2] The liveliness of this narrative manner is so great, and the progressive development of the themes so continuous, that various minor inconsistencies which are apparent to the attentive reader pass unnoticed by the hearer.

The subjective narrative manner, in which the poet himself interposes and speaks, is employed mainly in situations where certain explanations and comments are called for which cannot be conveyed by the objective narrative; for the poet who recites is obliged to anticipate the various questions which may arise in the minds of his hearers, and to supply the necessary details that will make the situations clear. Generally these interventions are brief, often so brief that they almost pass unnoticed. Only in rare instances are the personal interventions of the poet expanded so that sometimes they break the epic illusion.[3] This happens in

---

1.   Each of the first two narrative manners occupies about a fifth of the Iliad and the Odyssey while the third one occupies three fifths; v. Bassett 1938, 85.
2.   This is perhaps why Homeric presentations contain so many acoustic images.
3.   eg II, 811-814; 15, 224-255. These interventions often stimulate and assist the listener's participation in the events taking place (22, 32f; XV, 601-602; XVII, 278f) or prepare him for the announcement of a hero's death (as in the case of Sarpedon, Patroclus, Hector and Achilles). If the impending crisis arrives with-

V, 303f, for example, where the poet says that Diomedes hurled a stone at Aeneas so huge that not even two men "of our time" could lift it, and in 5, 335, where the poet tells us that Leucothea was once mortal, but that today she is one of the sea-goddesses: " . . . but now in the salt sea has been acknowledged by the gods."

In his personal interventions the poet addresses the Muse or Muses and Apollo, and four of the heros, by name: Menelaus, Melanippus and Patroclus in the Iliad, and Eumaeus in the Odyssey. All these interventions, naturally, are addressed obliquely to his hearers, since it is to them essentially that the poet is speaking, even though epic poetry normally is never addressed directly to the audience.[4] Among other things, these interventions give the listeners the respite they need in order to appreciate the significance of an important event by highlighting its seriousness or making some allusion to events that are to follow (cf 22, 32; XV, 601; XVII, 268).

The third, the dramatic narrative manner, is used widely and very successfully. By making the heroes speak in the first person, epic poetry succeeds in presenting them as living people who reveal their own inner world; and this element gives the narrative a unique life of its own. It was precisely for his use of dialogue and monologue that Homer was named the first of the tragic poets (Plato, *Republic* 394 B).

The speeches of the Homeric heroes are public and private. In their public speeches the leaders discuss or put forward their opinions in council and in the agora, or pass on official messages. In their private speeches the heroes argue among themselves, and exhort, provoke or abuse each other. In their speeches generally they express their feelings spontaneously, with a primitive eloquence drawn from life itself and not from book-learning. The whole personality of the hero emerges from his words endowed with life, and it is this quality rather than the force of his arguments that overmasters the person he is talking to. Furthermore,

---

out warning, then the poet addresses himself to the hero. In these cases the poet employs a word-indicator ($\tau \acute{o} \tau \epsilon, \tau o \tilde{v}, \acute{\epsilon} \nu \theta a$).

4.   In the case of epic poetry no 'gentle hearer' existed as, for example, in the 19th century novel. But it is obvious that the infrequent rhetorical questions are directed at an audience (eg XXII, 202f or 22, 12f), since there is no one else at whom they could be aimed.

the 'reasonable' arguments put forward are few and the antagonists never discuss or even examine them. In their speeches epic heroes simply state their opinions and expect their interlocutors to be immediately convinced. They rarely expound or analyse what they wish to say. What chiefly distinguishes them is their violence of emotion, and it is this that causes their dramatic clashes.

The style of the speeches is simpler than that of the narrative passages in the poem. In their speeches, especially the last lines, a number of gnomic statements can be found. Gnomes are among the most characteristic features of the Homeric epic. The wisdom of many generations is contained in their brief statements, and their pithy phrasing reveals a high moral tone.[5] But perhaps their greatest charm is their lack of any narrow, didactic element.[6]

The main purpose of the speeches of the Homeric heroes is to bring the different characters to life, but this does not mean that they play no other role in the narrative. They also assist the listener's imagination to visualize the hero's outward appearance (v. 68f) - a man who speaks in a certain manner should have an appearance to match - which is never directly described in the epic. Another of their functions is to spin out a scene so that the listener can appreciate it better, and so that, while what happened or what was said earlier is being repeated, the more important points in the narrative are recalled to the listener and given further emphasis.[7] The heroes' speeches often touch on things that are going to happen later, and so the audience is prepared in advance and is able to follow the course of the plot with greater ease (eg VIII, 473-476; XII, 113-115, etc.).

---

5. In the Iliad there are at least thirty such aphorisms, and many more in the Odyssey. In the Iliad these succinct gnomic statements and the similes occupy one line or less (V, 531; XII, 412), while in the Odyssey we find longer gnomes taking up two or more lines (8, 167f). Aeneas' speech to Achilles in XX 200-258 is perhaps the most full of them. It seems that the proclivity to gnomic moralization became stronger at the end of the epic tradition.
6. Sainte-Beuve compares the ethical teachings of Homer with a fountain in a Florentine garden, where the water pours from a vase held by Poseidon without the god being aware of what he is holding.
   On the speeches of Homeric heroes v. Blass 1887-1888, intro.; Croiset 1875; and cf Quintilian's admiration in *Inst. Orat.* X 1, 46.
7. The repetitions are commonest in the places where some injunction is given. Out of over 400 single speeches in both epics forty percent are commands.

The Homeric epics employ monologue as well as dialogue; there are some twenty examples of this (Hentze 1904, 12f). If the atmosphere is overcharged with emotion and a dialogue therefore becomes impossible, then the hero thinks aloud (eg III, 365-368; XXII, 297-305); 'Homer' in fact makes more use of direct speech than any other epic poet of the Western world.[8]

Consideration for the audience.

The poet's consideration for his hearers is, as we have seen, a basic factor in oral poetry, and it has to a great extent an influence on the narrative technique itself. The rhapsode's success or failure is apparent during the actual course of the recitation, and consequently the poet's primary concern is to keep a firm hold of his hearer's attention. It is natural, then, that he should try first and foremost to relieve his audience of the strain of any added mental effort and to keep them in a state of relaxed receptivity.[9] In order to achieve this, epic poetry developed directness, simplicity and fullness in its narrative, together with a dramatic manner of presenting the incidents it describes. Indeed this dramatic element characterizes not only the dialogue, but the whole structure of the Iliad and Odyssey, as well as the mode of presentation of different episodes.

Nevertheless we must not forget that Greek epic poetry, like Greek tragedy, drew its material from legends that were well known to its audience. Consequently the interest it sought to stimulate was different from that stimulated by the narrative poetry of later times, or the contemporary novel. It centred primarily on the manner in which the poet presented and developed his theme.

In the Odyssey, for example, the focus of interest is centred on the development of the complicated action and not on the outcome of the story, because everyone knew that Odysseus would eventually return to

8. cf Bassett 1938, 59. It is unnecessary to point out that many Homeric speeches are also uttered in part obliquely, especially in unimportant cases, eg in XI, 646.
9. From this point of view the poet's attitude toward his audience is like the orator's. We have only to think of Demosthenes (XIX, 340), who said that in most of the arts a man is relatively independent, but the art of oratory fails if the audience does not help the speaker.

his own country and find his faithful Penelope waiting for him there. The unknown factors in the Odyssey, therefore, are the means by which the hero will elude the various dangers, how he will put into effect his final plan, his disguise, the successive recognitions of him by his people, and his unmatched nimbleness of wit. It is in his treatment of these subjects that the epic poet has an opportunity to demonstrate his skill as a story-teller.

In the Iliad the unforeseen element and the hearer's interest depend on the Will of Zeus and the deferment of its fulfilment. Around this theme are woven the various digressions and additions, each of which would have been judged on its own merits. As the martial epic proceeded the audience knew beforehand who would be killed in every battle and who would survive, but that in no way lessened its interest. What was important was the hero's confrontation with the ineluctable. Another source of interest lay in the detailed descriptions of the wounding and deaths of the heroes.

Thus the epic shows us the sadness of death and the power of destiny, along with the profoundness of human frailty, because heroic deeds are presented as a strange alloy of divine determination and human effort, which is itself subject to the will of the gods. It is this that gives the Homeric epics their heroic, and at the same time their human character.

The poet's concern with his hearers is responsible both for his tendency to repeat incidents, motifs and themes, and also in part for the repetition of stock phrases. Many of these repetitions are designed, as we have seen, to protect the rhapsode from an unwanted break-down in the recital, but they are also due to the rhapsode's desire to assist his hearers' memory and relieve him of the need for any superfluous mental effort. The known and the familiar is always pleasant, whence the reason for many of the variations with which certain formulas are presented.

The same regard for his listener is displayed by the rhapsode when he tells in advance the outcome of the episode he is describing. So, in a way, the listener himself is made to assume the role of poet; in other words, he participates in the unfolding of the plot and is allowed to know, and to know in advance, everything known to the rhapsode himself

(Duckworth 1933). This is why he is told everything he needs to know either directly by the bard (cf VII, 445f and 473-476; XI, 192-194; XVI, 644-651, etc), or indirectly through the speeches of the heroes and gods. This advance knowledge, however, in no way diminishes the interest of the hearer in the continuation of the story, which, as we have seen, he knows in general lines right from the beginning.

The close relationship between the poet and his audience is also demonstrated by the absence of any explicit motivation for certain of the actions described in the epics. At many critical moments - a characteristic instance is in book XVI of the Iliad, where no explanation is given of the reasons why Achilles allows Patroclus to help the Achaeans, while he himself does not take part in the battle (Monro 1957[4], 307-308) - the poet omits to mention the reasons for certain things, and the listener is obliged to supply them himself. Often the heroes of the epic are depicted as knowing things which, according to the plot, they ought not to know, but about which the poet has already informed the audience. [10] Achilles, for instance, should not have known about Chryses' prayer to Apollo (I, 380, cf I, 35), and Patroclus should not have known about Sarpedon's first attack on the wall of the Greeks (XVI, 558, cf XII, 397f); and in many of the single-combats in the Iliad, the one adversary should not have known who the other was. Yet all these things are assumed to be known for the simple reason that the poet has already made them known to his listeners. In this way many tedious repetitions and explanations are avoided.

Finally, this same concern for the ease of his hearer causes the epic poet to state the name of every new character as soon as he is introduced, and, where possible, to relate him to the other characters in the story who are already known. [11]

---

10. As Fraccaroli (1903, 397. 400) noted, the only real and continuous relationship is that of the author with his reader; the relationship of the author with his heroes is ephemeral and does not exist outside of his imagination.
11. The one exception is Theoclymenus in the Odyssey, who is introduced in 15, 235 although his name is not mentioned until later, in 15, 256.

Some other important elements of epic technique.

The descriptive element is found widely distributed everywhere throughout the epic narrative, because the poet tries to paint a mental picture of every scene in the plot. [12] What is striking is not only the variety, but the clarity of the epic images, as well as the matchless technical skill of the narrative. With a few brush strokes the rhapsode brings an object, a person or a scene to life before our eyes, leaving the listener to fill in the blanks in the picture from his own imagination. In this way the listener has a creative share in the artistic experience. We may say, indeed, that perhaps no other form of Greek poetry has the suggestive power of the epic, or achieves such great results with such little apparent effort.

It has been said that "Homer" was a keen observer rather than a visualizer, and that this is the reason for his precise descriptions, as well as his knowledge about so many different matters - hunting and fishing, weaving and building, tactics, armament, medicine, etc. (Bucholtz 1871-5; Reichel, 1901).

This, in general, is true. Nevertheless, alongside the realistic descriptions of things and places we also find many synthetic descriptions in the epic, which for all their vividness and charm do not correspond to actual things. The use of many stock phrases with a fixed metrical position in the line caused elements of different things and from different periods to become associated; as a result, the epic depicts objects made up of different components which never co-existed in real life.

For example, we find a description of a helmet, which was not basically of metal, decorated with a horse's tail and reinforced with various other elements; the description had already become incomprehensible by the time the Homeric epics were acquiring their monumental form. This Homeric helmet is undoubtedly full of splendour and elaborate ornament, and therefore it makes a lively impression on the reader; but in the description new elements, taken from later helmets,

---

12.   Here I should like to stress once more that Homeric representations mainly use visual images, but they also use images that appeal to the senses of hearing, touch, smell and taste.

have been added without displacing the older elements. It follows that this type of helmet, as described in the Iliad, never existed in reality (Gray 1967, 62). Equally mixed up are many synthetic descriptions of shields,[13] and various descriptions of battles and chariots.

Battle descriptions, as one would expect, occupy a great part of the Iliad. However, their dominant characteristic is that, while the preliminaries - challenges, genealogies, taunts, etc. - are given detailed descriptions, the battles themselves are treated only in a very general way and given no special emphasis. Many engagements are no more than stereotyped skirmishes, with few variations - a sword breaking, for example, or a spear missing its target and killing another warrior. Usually the battles in the Iliad consist of a series of single-combats; rarely do we encounter a more general engagement.[14]

The heroes arrive at the battle ground in their chariots, driven by their faithful charioteers - the most important individuals so far as the warriors were concerned; they were normally kin or men of the household (Trypanis 1963) - and they then generally leap down from their chariots and fight as foot soldiers.[15] Nowhere in the Iliad do chariots appear marshalled in any battle array, while fights between two chariots only occur in three places, all in VIII (81f. 116f. 256f). We are also, indeed, offered the unlikely spectacle of three-horse chariots (VIII, 87 and XVI, 474), and even a four-horse chariot like those used in chariot racing (VIII, 185, cf 13, 81) ! From all of which we are forced to conclude that the use of chariots as described in the Homeric epics is a convention not related to reality. It would seem that the chariots referred to in the epics are primarily private and racing chariots, and are not the earlier, actual war-chariots of the Mycenean period (Delebéque 1951, 86).

---

13. In Homer shields of different periods are described, from the earliest Mycenean tower-shield to the round hoplite shield of the 7th century; v. Lorimer 1950, 132f.
14. The view has been expressed that battle descriptions with catalogues of the victims are an element of earlier heroic narrative; cf Lesky 1966, 39. The boulders which are used as weapons and which appear sporadically in the Homeric scenes, possibly represent the survival of an earlier epic component. On Homeric battles v. Fenik 1968.
15. Although the heroes usually jump down from their chariots to fight, there are often fights between a warrior on foot and another in a chariot; there are

This does not mean that in the earlier stages of epic tradition accurate descriptions did not exist of the two-horse chariot which, as we know from excavations, was Mycenean; the fossilized descriptive formulas associated with this kind of chariot are evidence that such descriptions really had existed in more ancient times (Page 1959, 280 n63). But in later periods, when war-chariots were no longer used as they had been in Mycenean times, the description of them as well as their actual function became mixed up with, and overlaid by descriptions of post-Mycenean and even Archaic racing chariots.

Apart from chariots, a number of other elements in the Iliad show that very often things described in the Homeric epics are outside the bounds of possibility. [16] Thus the Trojan attack on the Achaean camp encountered great difficulties so long as the wall and ditch were there to protect it. This is why, in VIII, we find the anti-chariot ditch disappearing and reappearing in accordance with the requirements of the moment. The same thing happens in the *Patrocleia* (XVI), where it is overlooked that Patroclus, who is presented fighting on foot, is riding in a chariot in lines 257f and 287f. Again horses, which never trample a dead body, "trample dead men and shields alike" in XX, 497f.

Such descriptions, which do not correspond with reality, are more obvious in the minor variations and the details of battle episodes, where they often verge on the fantastic, for all that they are given a deceptive cloak of realism (Wolf-Hartmut 1956). For example, in XVI, 612f (= XVII, 528f) a spear which has missed its target quivers as it sticks in the ground; in XIII, 442-444 the same image is used, but this time the spear sticks in the opponent's heart and then begins quivering to his heartbeats. Obviously the first can happen and the second cannot. I nevertheless think, although most critics, who condemn this passage precisely for

---

twenty such instances. Formulas like ἐξ ὀχέων . . . . σὺν τεύχεσιν, ἆλτο χαμᾶξε, καθ' ἵππων, ἀφ' ἵππων show that originally warriors avoided fighting from their chariots.

16. v. Delebécque 1951, 103f. As is natural, there are many topographical mistakes in the Homeric descriptions of Troy, but the account of the hot and cold springs in XXII 149-152 is correct. This shows that on the whole memories of Troy became blurred and inaccurate as they passed into legend; but the poet of Iliad XII, considered late on many grounds, appears to be well-informed about the Troad, and it is not unlikely that it was he who added lines 149-152 to XXII.

its lack of realism, would disagree, that the false imagery does in fact evoke a certain strange poetic emotion in the reader.

Single-combats have a place apart among the battles described in the Homeric epics and are, as we have seen, one of the common themes of epic tradition.[17] The principal single-combats - those of Menelaus and Paris (III), Hector and Ajax (VI), the *aristeia* of Diomedes (V), of Agamemnon (XI) and Menelaus (XVII), and the final great combat between Achilles and Hector (XXII) - play an important part in the structure and tone of the Homeric narrative: they are focal points within the action and, being complete and independent scenes, reflect more clearly the epic ideals.

It should further be noted here, as has been said above, that the exploits of a hero arouse greater admiration than the description of a crowded battle scene, the details of which are rapidly obscured; and that single-combat arouses a more interested response because it is a personal affair, and the clash of personalities is more clearly apparent. Finally, we must not overlook the hortative (didactic) element that is found in the exploits of the great heroes.

Let us now turn to the descriptions of persons, things and places, which have particular significance for an understanding of epic narrative technique. The first point to be stressed is that the epic never gives direct detailed descriptions of the splendid outward appearance of its heroes, but suggests it indirectly - the beautiful is never described. The only mortal to be fully described is Thersites (II, 216f),[18] who is a ludicrous person, and the poet takes a delight in emphasizing his ugliness and making fun of him.[19] Only in a very few instances does he give a descriptive detail about a hero's appearance, and then it is to make an ensuing

---

17. It has been maintained that all epic poetry began with short accounts of single-combats; v. Nitzsch 1862, 57. 356; Jaeger 1960, 44. I do not share this view; v. Trypanis 1963.

18. "He was the ugliest man that had come to Ilium. He had a game foot and was bandy-legged. His rounded shoulders almost met across his chest; and above them rose an egg-shaped head, which sprouted a few short hairs." (II, 216f). It is characteristic that in the Odyssey (13, 429-438) the detailed description of Odysseus' transformation into a beggar also produces a repulsive picture.

19. In the *Teichoscopia* in Iliad III, 161f, the poet had a wonderful opportunity to describe the external appearances of his heroes had he so wished. And yet

action or event more vivid, and not in order to describe the hero himself. We know, for example, that Hector had long black hair, only because his hair was dragged through the dirt behind Achilles' chariot (XXII, 401f); we also know that Achilles had fair hair, only because " . . . he cut from his head an auburn lock . . . " (XXIII, 140f) in order to dedicate it to the dead body of Patroclus.

Of especial interest is the indirect way epic poetry stimulates the hearer's imagination to form his own ideal image of each hero, and not to accept passively the one imposed by the poet were he to give detailed descriptions. In this way all the important heroes of the Homeric epics and many of the secondary ones are made to come alive before our eyes.

The indirect descriptive methods employed in the epic are 1) the *ethopoiia*, or the depiction of the characters through their own words and deeds (v. 60f). In an ideal heroic world like that of the epic, a man with a particular character will have an appearance to match it; therefore every hearer visualizes every hero according to his own conception of the heroic ideal; 2) the similes suggest vividly both the external appearance and the psychology of the hero. Achilles, for example, as he arrives near the walls of Troy, is compared with Sirius (XXII, 21f), which is the brightest star in the sky, but also the bearer of sorrow and sickness among men. Paris is compared to a proud horse galloping free across the plain (VI, 503-514), and Hector to a snake (XXII, 93-96). I will give two complete similes to illustrate the manner in which an image of the hero is suggested. In the first Ajax is defending Patroclus' body like a lion protecting its cubs (XVII, 132-137):

"Meanwhile Aias covered Patroclus with his broad shield and stood at bay, like a lion who is confronted by huntsmen as he leads his cubs through the forest, and plants himself in front of the helpless creatures, breathing defiance and lowering his brows to veil his eyes. Thus Aias planted himself by the lord Patroclus."

In the second, Idomeneus, who is awaiting Aeneas' attack, is compared to a wild boar (XIII, 470-477):

"But Idomeneus was not to be scared off like a little boy. He waited for him like a mountain boar when he is caught by a crowd of huntsmen in some lonely spot and faces the hue and cry with bristling back and eyes aflame, whetting his tusks in his eagerness to take on all comers, hound or man. Thus the renowned spearman Idomeneus awaited the onslaught of Aeneas and gave no ground at all."

3) The stock epithets - like "fleet-footed Achilles", "fair-haired Menelaus", etc. - refer to one of the hero's outward characteristics, but also indirectly suggest a great deal more. For instance, fair-haired Menelaus must have had not only fair hair, but blue eyes and a white skin; fleet-footed Achilles can only have had long, strong legs and a finely proportioned torso, and so forth.

The lack of detail in the descriptions of heroes accords with the fact that the Homeric heroes doubtless became stock figures early on in the epic tradition. This being the case, it was sufficient to make reference to a certain characteristic, and no more. This reference was not intended to be a description, but to identify each hero and distinguish him from the others. Something analogous may be seen in the medieval epic poem of Digenes Akritas, or even, in a way, in Christian iconography.[20]

Achilles' personality - and his only - is described in a particular manner, which emphasizes the splendour of his appearance and his exceptional attributes; I shall call this 'negative description', or the 'not so great as' manner. Achilles stands out from the other heroes of the Iliad, and this is emphasized in the comparisons between them. In other words, reference is often made to other heroes, who are characterized as brave, handsome, violent, etc., and these characterizations are then finished off with the phrase, "but not so excellent (handsome, brave, violent, etc.) as Achilles". Thus, as fresh characterizations are added, Achilles' appearance and personality are emphasized cumulatively and assume superhuman proportions[21] in the eyes of the reader (or hearer), without any direct description ever being given.

---

all he does is to repeat at slightly greater length the characteristic epithets used for each of them. Lines III, 203-224 about Odysseus were probably added after the composition of the Odyssey.

20. St George, for example, must always be portrayed as young and on horseback. The individual characteristics are quite unimportant.

21. eg in XVI, 707f: "Back, my lord Patroclus! The city of the lordly Trojans is not destined to be captured by your spear, nor even by Achilles, who is a far

It is noticeable that in all the accounts of people's outward appearances, the description of any sudden motion of the body that is not related to a change of place presents especial difficulty. It is therefore not surprising that epic poetry pauses at graphic moments which are vividly impressed on our memories: for instance, Thetis kneeling before Zeus, Priam falling at Achilles's feet, the hands of the wounded fighters stretched out in supplication. The more vivid movements are suggested but never described, or are illustrated by striking similes.

Epic poetry does not describe many of the things mentioned in the narrative. Palaces, clothes, equipment, ornaments, metal objects, etc., are presented for our admiration, not with a description of all their details, but with some general explanation, such as that they are the products of Phoenician craftsmanship, or the works of Hephaestus or Athena.

There are indeed certain notable exceptions, like Nestor's Cup, Heracles' baldric, Odysseus' boar's tusk helmet, or Agamemnon's breastplate. These are described in detail, but the main purpose of the descriptions is to emphasize how exceptional the objects are, and not really to tell us what they looked like. In other cases, where one might have expected a detailed description of particular things, like Agamemnon's sceptre, Achilles' great spear, or Odysseus' bow, almost nothing is said about them. On the other hand, we are given their histories, and more especially the histories of the persons connected with them. And this is in keeping with the spirit of the epic, which is more concerned with people than with things. This interest in people is apparent also in the descriptions of lesser warriors, as well as in many of the similes. In both cases another person's emotional reactions - man is still the central focal point (v. 60f) - are depicted, and this serves to heighten the interest and adds a lyrical touch. Thus, when Iphidamas is killed, he leaves behind him his "newly-wedded" wife (XI, 242-243); Bathycles, when he is killed, is described as "Chalcon's beloved son" (XVI, 594f); and when the moon is shining in the sky . . . and the wind is still, the shepherd is represented as "taking great delight", etc. .

We encounter the same technique in the Odyssey, where we are given a description, not of the splendid dance of the Phaeacians, but of the impression it made on the most important spectator, Odysseus (8,

71

264-266). We can see that Homeric poetry seeks rather to build up mental impressions of the people and things it describes than to give a detailed visual picture of them. This is obvious even in the description of Achilles' Shield (XVIII, 478-608), which is also the most important description of an object in the Homeric epics; we find no mention of the order in which the different representations are laid out on the shield; it is simply stated that Oceanus encircles them all. The poet also says nothing about the technical side of the masterpiece. Only the tools used by Hephaestus in his work are mentioned, and these are simple and primitive: bellows, crucibles, hammer, anvil and tongs; and there is mention of the metals used: bronze, silver, gold and tin. The scenes depicted on the famous shield - which are rightly considered to have a certain analogy with the Homeric similes - are all things known to the audience, and the allusion to Daedalus has no more than the sense of an epic superlative. Even the personifications that are depicted add nothing to the descriptions. It is clear that the poet is seeking to arouse in the listener the emotions engendered by war and peace rather than to describe realistically the scenes which engender them; basically it amounts to no more than a wider, more general perspective of life, in which the Trojan war is also being enacted. There is indeed so much movement in these images - the poet, in other words, explains in such detail what the figures portrayed on the shield are doing - that one cannot conceive of them as representing an actual description of a static work of art.[22]

Homeric poetry lays very little importance on the locality where most of the episodes take place; we are never given a general description of the landscapes in which the different scenes are enacted. Only foreign places, which would naturally arouse more curiosity, are described in somewhat more detail. We are told more, for example, about the land of the Cyclopes than about the camp of the Achaeans on the Trojan plain, where all the great battles of the Iliad take place.

---

better man than you." Also, XVII, 278f: " . . . Aias, who next to the peerless son of Peleus was the finest Danaan of all in looks and the noblest in action." In XXIII, 791 it is said of Odysseus that "it's a hard job to beat him in a race - for any of us but Achilles." And in XVIII. 54f Thetis laments, "Ah misery me, the unhappy mother of the best of men. I brought him into the world a flawless child to be a mighty hero . . . " etc. .

22. This *ecphrasis*, that is the description in verse of a work of art, forms the beginning of a long, and noble tradition in Greek poetry, which has lasted into our own times, for example in the famous description of the Parthenon by Kostes Palamas in *The King's Flute*.

There is particular interest in the descriptions of the 'urban' environment in the Odyssey, such as the palace of Alcinous on Scheria. It shows some advance as compared with the Iliad, and this is due in part to the subject matter of the Odyssey itself. Equally interesting are the descriptions of 'idyllic landscapes' such as Calypso's Cave (5, 63-74), the garden of Alcinous (7, 112-132), or the harbour of Phorcys (13, 96-112), which bring a new poetic note to the epic. The idyllic peace and beauty of the descriptions mark the beginning of a new trend in Greek poetry, which reaches its peak in Hellenistic times with the idylls of Theocritus.

Now let us take a closer look at the Homeric similes, which are one of the most admirable features of epic poetry. In the Iliad there are 182 fully developed similes, while in the Odyssey there are only 39. They introduce everyday life into the lofty heroic world. It could be said that they are the earthly roots of Homeric poetry, because not only do they refer to matters known at first hand to the audience, they are also directly aimed at the hearer's senses. The images employed allow us to see, hear, touch, smell and taste everything they deal with. They raise us above the narrow, local confines of the heroic world, and set the events of the battle-field in a wider temporal perspective. We are aware of life rolling onwards independently of the war, both before and after the war, and it is this quality, for all that it only appears occasionally and sporadically, that makes the similes come alive in the telling.

In the similes the theme is stated first, then the place (some 150 instances), and more rarely the time (some 10 instances). Details are also given which are quite irrelevant to the matters being compared, [23] and lastly, the feelings evoked by the images are very often explicitly stated. What makes great poetry of the similes is that they are centred around the human factor. In IV, 452, where the oncoming warriors are compared to two winter torrents meeting in spate and pouring down the mountainside, the image is completed by the phrase, " . . . and far off in the hills a shepherd hears their thunder." In VIII, 555f, where the watch-fires of the Trojans are compared with the stars shining all around the moon on a still, cloudless night, the image is completed by

---

23. In fact in the Homeric epics, unlike the rationalist Apollonius Rhodus, the *tertium comparationis* does not play a major role. One of the best observations about the Homeric similes was made by the ancient scholiast (Schol. T on XII 41), who said that the extra details included in the similes added nothing to the comparisons but served as poetical embellishments.

the phrase, " . . . when every star is seen, and the shepherd rejoices."

The Homeric similes embrace many and diverse matters.[24] They
speak of the changing seasons, the clearness of starry nights, clouds
rolling by, full moons, the evening star, Sirius, thunder-storms and
mountain torrents swollen by the rains, great forest fires, the smoke
rising from a burning city, the eternal sea-changes. Just as powerful are
the scenes drawn from wildlife: lions attacking wild boars, swooping
falcons, or a wounded deer at the mercy of a hound. And there are
scenes from everyday life: a mother shooing the flies away from her
child, a woman painting ivory red to use in a horse's bridle, men
harvesting, boys beating a donkey, a child building sand-castles, the
potter working his wheel, woodcutters adzing the trunk of a tree to
make a ship from its planks, etc. .

Each of these similes - and we have mentioned only a small selection - has its lyricism. The images, taken from humble, daily life, show
in an indirect fashion that the heroic, warlike existence is not everything, and that often its real worth is only appreciated when it is compared with something more simple and homely.[25] It may be added
that certain subjects, such as large human crowds in movement, can only
be rendered with vigour and conciseness by similes.[26]

Linguistic studies of the Homeric epics have shown that later
linguistic elements are often embedded in the similes, and this has led a
number of scholars to believe that the similes belong to the later stages
of epic tradition (Shipp 1953, 18f). This conclusion, they say, applies
mainly to the fully developed similes, where the aim is to depict an object in its entirety, in the course of which even features quite irrelevant
to the comparison are introduced; and it applies also to the double
similes.[27] Certainly it is difficult to believe that the many small similes
(the formulas, composed of a single phrase not exceeding half a line)

24. It is rare for a simile to be repeated in its entirety (as eg VI, 506-511 = XV,
     263-269).
25. There are no similes in Homer that are out of keeping with epic decorum. On
     the Homeric similes v. Finsler 1918-1924 I, 2, 258f; Cauer 1921, 459f; Fränkel
     1921.
26. We find such instances in II, 87f. 145f. 465f; XIII, 334f.
27. The double simile probably appeared in the epics after the first written
     versions, in other words when different variations and parallels were written

belong to the later stages of the epic. This view, however, that the similes are late features of epic tradition, is countered by the fact that in the Odyssey, which is the later of the two poems, we have far fewer of them than in the Iliad.

Finally it should be pointed out that sometimes the comparison assists the hearer to comprehend some great thing he has never seen or experienced, by showing him something lesser with which he is familiar. For example, in XXI, 361 of the Iliad, the waters of the river Xanthus, as they boil from the fires kindled by Hephaestus, are compared with the water boiling in a common cauldron.[28]

Metaphor is very rarely employed in the Homeric epics.[29] This is a blessing, because excessive use of metaphor leads to artificiality and pompousness of style. The reason it is seen so seldom is that Greek epic poetry, in the process of stereotyping its phrases, deprives the words of any metaphorical sense and gradually transforms them into simple epic words and usages which in no way differ from any ordinary phrase (Parry 1933, 30f).

Let us take two common kinds of Homeric metaphor: 1) the stock metaphor limited to a single word,[30] and 2) the metaphor that is

----

down in the texts alongside the original similes, so that the rhapsodes could choose which of them to use. Later both versions became incorporated into the text and thus the double simile was created. This is clearly the case with II, 144-149 and II, 455-483.

28. The Alexandrian scholars were the first to notice that certain things, such as horsemanship, the use of the trumpet and the boiling of meat, occur in the Iliad only in the similes (Schol. Il. XV 679); XVIII 219; XXI 632). It has also been observed that Homeric heroes live on roast meat and eat fish only under great duress. Nevertheless in the similes fishing is represented as being a daily occurrence (Lesky 1947, 18).

29. v. Meister 1921, 244 n. 1. Aristotle had a great admiration for Homeric metaphor (*Rhetoric* 1411 B 31). The Byzantines also frequently referred to Homer's metaphors.

30. Here for example belong the words "κάρηνα", meaning heads for peaks (I, 44), the fast sailing ship which "ἔθεεν", coursed, the impudence which is worn like a garment, "ἀναιδείην ἐπιειμένε" (I, 149), etc. . The use of words like these is common, without there being any indication that the poet is consciously using them metaphorically.

75

expressed by a stock epithet.[31] We see immediately how frequent 'stock use' deprives them of any real metaphorical sense.[32] There are also some metaphors which go beyond the one word, but here too the formulaic factors - keeping the same position in the line and the same rhythm - turn them into regular epic phrases with no true metaphorical significance.[33]

There are, however, a few metaphors in the Homeric epics which preserve their metaphorical sense, such as the praise of Nestor's speech in I, 249 of the Iliad. Aristotle (*Rhetoric,* 1411 B 31) especially praises the Homeric metaphors which move "from the living to the lifeless", like the one in Iliad XI, 574, where the spears that miss their target and stick in the ground desire to gorge themselves on human flesh, " . . . and many another without tasting his white flesh fell short and stuck in the ground, balked of the feast it craved." Similarly in Odyssey 11, 598, where Sisyphus' boulder is called "shameless", " . . . and the shameless rock came bounding down again to level ground."

Naturally antiquity, particularly in the latter part, regarded Homer's every word and phrase as sacred. So what the Homeric metaphors had lost in liveliness as a result of the oral recitation of the epics over the centuries, they gained in the admiration and respect of their hearers or readers.

Another important characteristic of Homeric narrative is its singular conception of time. Since things that happen simultaneously cannot be simultaneously told, they are described consecutively in the epic. In

31. To these belong the "'ροδοδάκτυλος 'Ηώς" (rosy-fingered Dawn) (I, 477), the "χαλκοχίτωνες 'Αχαιοί" (bronze-shirted Achaeans) (I, 371), the "βοῶπις 'Ηρη" (ox-eyed Hera) (I, 568), etc. .
32. The phrase "ἔπεα πτερόεντα" (winged words), for example, occurs one hundred and twenty-three times in Homer, and "ροδοδάκτυλος 'Ηώς" (rosy-fingered Dawn) twenty-seven times. The choice of these words was certainly made largely for metrical reasons. And when a word is used only - or mainly - in order to help out the meter, its choice is not truly dictated by the meaning it conveys.
33. The "ὑγρὰ κέλευθα" (watery ways), for example, is often used at the end of a line as a formula (I, 312; 3, 71; 4, 842; 9, 252; 15, 474). But Homer also calls the sea "ἰχθυόεντα κέλευθα" (the fishy ways) and "ἠερόεντα κέλευθα" (windy ways). In none of these instances would the hearer have been able to grasp the metaphorical sense unless he paused to think.

such cases the poet sometimes explains - and very often does not - their actual chronological relationship.[34] In XV, 154f, Iris and Apollo have to carry out simultaneously the missions Zeus has given them: and yet in the narrative they are described as if they had actually carried them out one after the other (cf XV, 222f). Thus epic poetry proceeds with its narrative as though there were no chronological unity to which all the events should be referred; time is used only as a measure of the duration of each particular incident.

Nevertheless, in this matter also the Odyssey appears to have progressed farther than the Iliad. In general it follows the rule of the consecutive narrative of two simultaneous events.[35] In certain instances, however, it changes scene twice,[36] a fact which also implies a different conception of time. But this narrative method often produces confusion, and its use is artificial (Page 1955, 68).

Also noteworthy are the first attempts at chronology that we find in the epics. It is true that what is described there belongs to the 'heroic period', which is set in a distant past, in a place and time far removed from the poet's. Within this vague, general setting, however, can be detected a first attempt at a chronology based on generations. We have two mythological cycles, the Trojan and the Theban, representing two successive generations. Diomedes and his charioteer, for instance, who fought at Troy, are the sons of the heroes who fought with the Seven against Thebes.

But perhaps most important of all is the fact that poetry was looking beyond individual events in themselves, and trying to relate them to life and the world as a whole; in other words, it was searching for the causal links and connections between things, and the deeper meaning that lies behind the march of events. If we look at the Homeric epics from this standpoint, we have to admit that Homer was rightly named the 'Father of History' (a title that was also, as a matter of fact,

---

34. Virgil, for example, who uses the same method, says at the beginning of the ninth book of the *Aeneid*: "Atque ea diversa penitus dum parte geruntur" (while these things are happening in a quite different place).
35. Thus Telemachus' journey (1-4) and the wanderings of Odysseus (5-13) are synchronous events, but in the narrative they are presented as following one after the other.

77

bestowed on Herodotus). In this field, too, the epic laid the foundations on which the Greeks were later to base all their historical enquiry.

------

36. In 15, 14-15 we move from Odysseus to Telemachus, and then in 15, 300 we move back from Telemachus to Odysseus, only to move back once again to Telemachus in 15, 494.

CHAPTER FIVE – MEN AND GODS IN THE HOMERIC EPICS

The world of men.

The Homeric epics operate on two planes, which form entirely separate worlds - the world of men and the world of gods. Happiness, joy and immortality riegn in the second, while misfortune, war and death dominate the first.

As we have said above, in the Iliad and Odyssey life is represented as being much richer than it really was during the last phase of the epic tradition. In war the Homeric heroes rejoice in their bronze arms, which are often decorated with gold, silver and enamel, are proud of their horses, follow a strict code of etiquette, and sacrifice many animals to the gods at their festivals. Away from the camp their palaces and orchards, furniture and clothes take on an exceptional splendour. And the heroes themselves, who are given human and not superhuman dimensions in the Homeric epics - the humanization of the myths and legends is perhaps the epics' greatest achievement - also exhibit a higher nobility.

The Homeric world of men - which differs in certain respects in the two poems - is itself one of the synthetic pictures created by epic tradition; it is made up of elements which often come from very diverse historical periods, beginning with the Mycenean and extending into the early Archaic period.

The society portrayed in the Homeric epics consists of the people ($\lambda\alpha o\iota$ = the soldiers), and they are ruled over by sceptred kings ($\sigma\kappa\eta\pi\tau o\tilde{\upsilon}\chi o\iota \beta\alpha\sigma\iota\lambda\tilde{\eta}\epsilon\varsigma$). The most powerful king summons the people to the 'agora'. But the crowds that come to these gatherings do not take part in the discussions or the decision-making. The leaders alone speak and decide, while the crowd occasionally expresses its feelings by a 'murmur' or by shouting. (I, 22; II, 271. 333. 394; VII, 403-404; XIX, 74f).

On only one occasion (II, 225f) does a member of the crowd, Thersites, speak up impudently and demagogically - a fact indicating

79

that this part of the Iliad is later - and then Odysseus forcibly compels him to be silent, and he sits down in his place, ". . . and in his pain looked round him helplessly and brushed away a tear."

In that early society the rules of war were brutal, and prisoners became slaves unless their kin put down a large ransom to free them.[1] A number of Asiatic elements can also be detected, expecially among the Trojans. Priam, for example, has many wives. Hecuba, indeed, holds the chief place, but Laothoe is also a person of honour, because her father gave her a great dowry when she married (XXII, 51).

One of the most charming aspects of this society is its respect for the guest. The bonds of hospitality are so powerful that the warriors will even stop fighting when they realize that their adversary has been their guest - as we can see in the well-known encounter between Glaucus and Diomedes in Iliad VI.

The Odyssey, naturally, tells us more about the peaceful side of life. On Ithaca we find a kind of local feudal system. Penelope's suitors are wealthy landowners with an eye on Odysseus' property. They amuse themselves in their palaces, but they also set ambushes for their enemies or to increase their wealth, and have their own private ships and retainers (4, 669-671; v. Finley 1956).

Life on the island of the Phaeacians is rather different; the authority is patriarchal. King Alcinous summons the leaders of the Phaeacians to inform them of his decisions about Odysseus, and offers him lavish hospitality. But the way of life is fairly simple, because we see Nausicaa, the king's daughter, going with the girls of the house to the river to wash the family's clothes, and queen Arete herself supervising the slave-women who heat the water for their guest's bath. Another interesting sidelight is the place of honour given to the bard ($\grave{\alpha}o\iota\delta\acute{o}\varsigma$) in the Odyssey; it shows that the profession of bard has progressed since the time of the Iliad.

The wives of the Homeric heroes are represented as beautiful noblewomen, wearing rich clothes, diadems ($\check{\alpha}\mu\pi\upsilon\xi$) on their heads, (XXII. 469) fillets ($\grave{\alpha}\nu\alpha\delta\acute{\epsilon}\sigma\mu\eta$) about their temples, and veils ($\kappa\rho\acute{\eta}\delta\epsilon\mu\nu\upsilon\nu$)

1. cf XXII 44-50 for example. Only in XXIV is there talk of ransom for the body of a dead warrior.

with which they could also cover their faces (1, 334) - another Eastern trait - and naturally they are bedecked with much gold jewellery. The women of this Homeric society have inherited from the Cretan and Mycenean civilizations a refined taste and fondness for luxury. In the epics woman's real *arete* is her beauty, even though her social and legal status makes her mistress of her household, and people honour her for her virtue and prudence. It is clear from the scene of the Viewing from the Walls (III, 156f) that the Trojans respect and honour Helen, for all that she has brought ruin on their country.

As for the children, they grow up in the wealthy Homeric households surrounded by their parents' love like many children of our own time: their fathers play with them (XXII, 500), they consume unlimited titbits (XXII, 504), and nannies put them to bed (XXII, 501-504). In all these aspects of their life there is nothing primitive or barbarous to be seen.

When we turn to the personalities depicted in the Homeric epics, we find ourselves astonished by their variety, ranging from the most savagely violent to the tenderest and most humane. In certain scenes the passions are recounted of primitive men who are ruled by their instincts. Such 'heroes' fight only for plunder; the purpose of their raiding is to sieze cattle, horses and women. Achilles himself, during the time of his great anger with Agamemnon, says that he bears no grudge against the Trojans, because "they have never lifted cow or horse of mine, nor ravaged any crop that the deep soil of Phthia grows to feed her men; for the roaring of the seas and many a dark range of mountains lie between us." (I, 154-157).

Quarrels are provoked by the unfair distribution of the spoils (I, 163-168). They readily let fly heated insults - Achilles calls Agamemnon "shameless", "self-interested", "dog-faced", and in his blind rage against Hector shouts that he would happily eat his flesh raw. Nor do they ever feel pity for the conquered adversary. Not only did Achilles drag Hector's dead body behind his chariot, but the other Achaeans also rushed to dishonour it with their spears.

Nevertheless, alongside these cruel scenes we find others full of the most delicate feeling and profound humanity. In the whole of epic poetry there is nothing to compare with Priam's speech when he comes to Achilles' tent to offer ransom for his son's body:

> "Most worshipful Achilles, think of your own father, who is the same age as I, and so has nothing but miserable old age ahead of him . . . .
> Yet he at least has one consolation. While he knows that you are still alive, he can look forward day by day to seeing his beloved son come back from Troy; whereas my fortunes are completely broken. I had the best sons in the whole of this broad realm, and now not one, not one I say, is left . . . .
> Most of them have fallen in action, and Hector, the only one I still could count on, the bulwark of Troy and the Trojans, has now been killed by you, fighting for his native land. It is to get him back from you that I have come to the Achaean ships, bringing the princely ransom with me. Achilles, fear the gods, and be merciful to me, remembering your own father, though I am even more entitled to compassion, since I have brought myself to do a thing that no one else on earth has done - I have raised to my lips the hand of the man who killed my son." (XXIV, 486f)

Achilles' reply is no less moving (XXIV, 517f), as Priam's words soften his heart and lift him above his anger, and pity floods into his heart - not only for the old man who has kissed the hand that killed so many of his sons, but for the whole of mankind, which suffers under the indifferent gaze of the gods.

Marital and paternal tenderness are painted with a similar power in the farewell between Hector and Andromache in Iliad VI, where Andromache says to Hector:

> "So you, Hector, are father and mother and brother to me, as well as my beloved husband. Have pity on me now; stay here on the tower; and do not make your boy an orphan and your wife a widow . . . . "
> (VI, 429f)

And Hector replies:

> "All that, my dear, is surely my concern. But if I hid myself like a coward and refused to fight, I could never face the Trojans and the Trojan ladies in their trailing gowns . . . .
> Deep in my heart I know the day is coming when holy Ilium will be

destroyed, with Priam and the people of Priam of the good ashen spear.
Yet I am not so much distressed by the thought of what the Trojans
will suffer, or Hecabe herself, or King Priam, or all my gallant brothers
whom the enemy will fling down in the dust, as by the thought of you,
dragged off in tears by some Achaean man-at-arms to slavery."

Having said this, Hector wished to take his son in his arms,

> "But the child shrank back with a cry to the bosom of his girdled nurse,
> alarmed by his father's appearance. He was frightened by the bronze of
> the helmet and the horsehair plume that he saw nodding grimly down
> at him. His father and his lady mother had to laugh. But noble Hector
> quickly took his helmet off and put the dazzling thing on the ground.
> Then he kissed his son, dandled him in his arms, and prayed to Zeus and
> the other gods . . . . " (VI, 429f).

Hector's thoughts, while he is waiting to confront Achilles in the
last great single-combat of the Iliad, are yet another example of the
mastery with which the epic traces the interplay of thoughts and
emotions (XXII, 99-130). This monologue, in which Priam's son weighs
all the arguments for and against the single-combat with Achilles, is a
forerunner of the monologue which Attic tragedy was later to carry to
such a pitch of perfection.

Epic poetry manifests the same mastery in its descriptions of
female psychology. Among the female characters it is worth pausing at
Nausicaa, Alcinous' daughter. She not only has the daintiness and mod-
esty that are proper to every young girl, but she also possesses courage
and kindness. She is the only one of the group who does not run away in
terror when Odysseus suddenly appears naked among the girls who are
playing ball with her. She shows an equally well developed intelligence
when she says to him:

> "Sir, your manners prove that you are no rascal and no fool; and as for
> these ordeals of yours, they must have been sent by Olympian Zeus, who
> follows his own will in dispensing happiness to people whatever their
> merits. You have no choice but to endure. But since you have come to
> our country and city here, you certainly shall not want for clothing or
> anything else that an unfortunate outcast has the right to expect from
> those he approaches." (6, 187-193)

Nausìcaa gives the stranger clothing and whatever else he needs, and guides him to the city. She has, however, the presence of mind not to cause comment by walking through the streets with an unknown man. This female figure is the forerunner of the brave and noble maiden figures who are later portrayed with such power in Attic tragedy.

We have, of course, only mentioned a few of the many scenes displaying profound awareness of human feelings and a wonderful understanding of complex psychology, to use a modern term.

This contrast between violent primitive emotions and refined, evolved responses is one more indication that the composition of the Homeric epics is not a single work. It does in fact show different stages in the social and political development of the Greeks. Homeric emotions begin in a world of egoistical self-interest and unbridled instinctive passions, and end up at that point where men and women have achieved peaceful reflection and are capable of experiencing tenderness and pity.

Let us now look more closely at the three most important heroes of the Homeric epics; Achilles, Hector and Odysseus; this will help us to a better understanding both of the ideals of the heroic period and the way in which they developed. In order to understand Achilles and his actions, however, we must first say a few words about heroic *arete,* or valour in battle, which is the ideal embodied to a greater or lesser extent in all the epic heroes; the fearless man is also the noble man, the man of high birth, and battle and victory constitute the highest distinction, the real purpose of life in the heroic epics. Hence the essence of Homeric *arete* is outstanding physical and mental strength, and it lacks the ethical content of chivalry as we find it in the Middle Ages.

In accordance with this older ideal, the epic hero must excel in his every action. The line "Let your motto be I lead. Strive to be best . . . " (VI, 208) sums up wonderfully the essence of this most ancient Greek aristocratic *arete.*

This meaning of *arete* is closely linked to the notion of honour (τιμή) - the honour which everyone possessing *arete* is entitled to enjoy. To be deprived of honour was the greatest human misfortune that could befall a member of the epic aristocracy. The more important the hero, the greater his thirst for honour, because honour belongs to human achievement and proves not only to society but to the hero himself what he is really worth.[2] Honour and dishonour, therefore, emanate from the praise or censure of one's fellow men. And since the *arete* shown by a hero during his lifetime will continue to live on in the memory of his achievements after his death, praise was the only means by which the epic warrior could achieve 'immortality.'

Thus the tragic conflict between Achilles and Agamemnon in the Iliad should be seen as an expression of heroic *arete,* and judged according to the primitive aristocratic code of that age. Achilles' calamitous anger and his refusal to help the Achaeans has no analogy with a modern man's desire for honour, nor does it betoken a lack of patriotism - which was unknown at that time as we know it today - nor should it be regarded simply as the obstinacy of a man who has no sense of proportion. Achilles' desire for honour is commensurate with his heroic status and is entirely in keeping with the sentiments of the aristocracy of that distant age.

An appeal to the hero's patriotism, which in later times might have brought a solution to the 'wrath', was something still quite unknown at that time. Agamemnon, in order to maintain command over his forces and keep them united, only invokes his rights as a despotic leader, and makes no appeal to a sense of racial solidarity, or to any feeling of his soldiers that they all shared a common homeland. Only by keeping this heroic code firmly in our minds can we understand the ideal which gave birth to Achilles and all the other great Homeric heroes.

Nevertheless, Achilles as we find him in the Iliad is something more than just an overbearing, ferocious hero. The earlier monolithic figure was little by little overlaid by, or rather expanded into, a more advanced heroic type. We can see this most clearly, perhaps, in Iliad IX -

----

2.   cf Aristotle, *Nicomachaean Ethics* A 3, 1095 B 26: "Moreover men's motive in pursuing honour seems to be to assure themselves of their own merit; at least they seek to be honoured by men of judgement and by people who know them, that is they desire to be honoured on the ground of virtue." With the growth of philosophical thought a personal, subjective scale of values came to determine a man's worth. The honour that was then shown to a person reflected his worth without being the actual source of it.

which in its present form is a 'later' book - where the heroic ideal is not restricted just to the man who is effective in action, but encompasses the man who is effective in speech. In this way an intellectual element is introduced and given a place of equal honour with valour in battle, and this fact throws some light on the later development of the epic. This is why, when Achilles' old tutor, Phoenix, tries to persuade the sulking hero to join in the fight again, he says to him:

"Did not the old charioteer Peleus make me your guardian . . . .
to teach you all these things, to make a speaker of you and a man of action . . . . " (IX, 438f)

To be a fine speaker and also to achieve great deeds - this summed up the later heroic ideal.

This new ideal, it has been observed, presupposes not only public debating in the camp, but the fully developed ancient city, the city-state, in which the gift of oratory was as important a weapon in political argument as the spear or sword in war.[3]

But the Achilles of Iliad IX is not yet ready to give way. He is prevented by the inflexible, primitive Achilles who stands behind him. He refuses all the royal gifts that are offered him, and demands recompense in the same coin for the bitter insult he has suffered; for originally no other payment could be made except in the same coin - humiliation for humiliation. The same attitude was taken by Ajax, for example, who was maddened by his dishonour, and who remained obdurate even in Hades, and kept himself far away from Odysseus (11, 543f). And Thetis, when she went to Zeus, asked that her son be paid back in the same coin; and Zeus, father of men and gods, assents:

"Zeus, as he finished, bowed his sable brows. The ambrosial locks rolled forward from the immortal head of the King, and high Olympus shook."[4]
(I, 528-530)

---

3. The Achilles of IX is depicted as a much more evolved type of person than the Achilles of I; this is clear from the Embassy scene in which Ajax, Odysseus and Phoenix find him singing "of famous men" and playing the phorminx.
4. These are the well-known lines said to have inspired Pheidias in his creation of the great gold and ivory statue of Zeus at Olympia.

Nevertheless, in the Iliad as we have it today, Achilles does give way in the end, and returns to the battle. But what makes him yield is not the royal gifts (which, incidentally, he does accept in XIX), nor the feeling that Agamemnon and the other Greeks have been sufficiently paid back for the insult he received, but the death of Patroclus, his closest friend.

We mentioned earlier the motif of close friendship and we need not therefore enlarge on it here (v. 14f). It will be enough to recall that this mythological and epic theme requires a man to sacrifice everything for his friend's sake, because this is the only way an epic hero can maintain his self-respect.

In fact, for the sake of Patroclus, Achilles sacrifices the very two things which the heroic, epic world held most precious - his honour and his life. He returns to the battle without having received proper satisfaction for the insult, and he knows - because Thetis has warned him of it so many times - that if he kills Hector he himself will die within a very short time.

And so the dark, egoistical anger of Achilles, which had such bitter consequences for the Achaeans and for the hero himself - for it brought about Patroclus' death - gave way to a nobler sentiment, the desire to avenge the death of a friend. In the course of this later remodelling of the Iliad, Achilles outgrew the original egocentric hero required by the Wrath theme, and developed into a more complex personality; he became capable of 'giving', and even of achieving self-sacrifice, for all that his desire for revenge was just as fierce as before.

In the end even his passion for blind revenge weakens and is replaced by something nobler, a feeling of compassion when he sees Hector's old father lying at his feet, and kissing the hand that has killed so many of his sons - the old father, who reminds him of his own father, Peleus. And this new Achilles, compassionate as the Old Father motif requires at this point, gives to the old father, Priam, Hector's body to bury. This scene has a tragic grandeur unique in Western literature. Behind this Achilles, however, there always looms the fierce egocentric, primitive hero, without whom the Iliad as we know it today would never have attained its unique, tragic depth or its singular poetic power.

Now we can turn to the question which has aroused so much controversy:[5] whether any moral development is perceptible in Achilles' character as the Iliad advances towards its conclusion. I am sure that Achilles, like many other heroes in the Iliad, had already become a stock figure by the time the epic acquired its monumental form. Consequently, in common with all traditional figures, he possessed certain fixed attributes which could not be omitted, radically altered or further elaborated.[6] Thus Achilles is the handsomest, the fleetest of foot, the doughtiest warrior, as well as a man whose emotions - his hatreds and loves - surpass those of other people in both intensity and partiality.

As the epic narrative unfolds, these stock types pass on from one scene to the next with all their principal attributes essentially unchanged, but acting in accordance with the particular requirements of each scene, each epic theme. This happens too with Achilles in the Iliad, where he has a principal role in the four basic epic themes we have considered - the Wrath, the Revenge, the Single-combat and the Old Father - which constitute the bones of the plot. In the Wrath theme the hero has to be portrayed as intransigent, and his thirst for honour must come before everything else. In the Revenge theme what must predominate, even at the cost of his thrist for honour, is the duty to avenge the death of his friend (or clan member). In the Single-combat he has to defeat his opponent, however mighty the man may be. And finally, in the Old Father theme, reverence for the old father must take first place, over and above his thirst for personal honour and blind passion for revenge.

Achilles, like every other epic hero, must conform to the requirements of each epic theme in which he is the protagonist. Yet in all four of the cases we have examined he always remains basically the same Achilles of tradition; the mighty warrior with violent emotions, the unvanquished and the hot-tempered - even in the Old Father theme in Iliad XXIV he is portrayed as losing his patience for a moment and threatening to show the same 'respect' to Priam that he has shown to

5.   Wilamowitz, for example, maintains that it makes no sense to speak of development in a character that is not the creation of one poet (1920, 251f). On the other hand Schmid - Stählin (1929, 95) believe that moral development is clearly discernible.

6.   They are restricted by the technique and aims of epic poetry, as well as by the 'simplicity' of heroic virtues and faults.

Hector - displays no signs of any real moral progress. Consequently, the humanity he exhibits in XXIV does not denote a conscious change in Achilles' character, effected by the composer of the monumental Iliad. It is due to the juxtaposition of the four basic epic themes we have described, which makes it necessary for Achilles to assume a different manifestation. This, and not a deliberately conscious modification of Achilles' character in the final composition of the epic, is what makes the Iliad the first great monument of Western humanism. If, however, the poet who presented the Wrath theme in its 'original' form could see the Iliad we have today, he would most probably find the work weak and degenerate. For, according to his own heroic code, the τιμή and ἀρετή of the great warrior has to predominate and take precedence over any form of love or compassion.

The epic hero is, in fact, great only when he defeats an important adversary; and Hector, Achilles' chief adversary, is such a one. Hector himself, however, is modelled after quite a different ideal. He is also, of course, a great and noble warrior, but he stands for more than just Trojan valour. He represents the new ideal of heroism, which is closely linked to the citizen's duty towards his country and family. In this new ideal we can see the rise of the city-state in the Greek world - as it came into being after the Mycenean period - and the place the family is beginning to take in peoples' lives.[7]

In Hector we see, besides the great warrior - who also has some very primitive traits[8] - a moving human figure at the moment when he is saying goodbye to his wife and playing tenderly with his child. He shows, furthermore, exceptional respect for his mother and great courtesy towards Helen. Everything about him makes us like Hector; we see in him all the beauty and sorrow of the doomed son and husband, father and patriot. Above all, however, he is the protector of Troy, and his death signifies the end of his country. We know that with his fall the Trojans will be destroyed; this is what makes the Iliad a real 'Iliad' and not just an 'Achilleid', or an epic celebrating the exploits of many great heroes.

---

7. Mycenae, like other similar centres in the Mycenean period, was not a city in the literal sense, but the fortified home of a warrior king.
8. In XVII, 125f he drags away Patroclus' body to cut off the head and throw it to the Trojan dogs, and in XVIII, 176f he wants to impale Patroclus' head on a stake.

Odysseus is the central figure in the Odyssey, an epic which is not far removed from a novel; it is rooted on the one hand in the heroic world of the past, and on the other in the world of myth and sea adventures. Odysseus' chief characteristic is stated directly in the first line of the epic:

> "The hero of the tale which I beg the Muse to help me tell is that resourceful man . . . . ''

But perhaps prudence is his greatest quality, clever, noble and strong though he is. The warrior of Troy lives on in the Odysseus of the Odyssey. How otherwise could he wipe out all his wife's suitors on Ithaca and defeat the Phaeacian athletes in the games? And yet these demonstrations of courage and strength do not appeal to our imaginations so much as his wonderful resourcefulness. He is the man who can escape from every impasse by his mental agility, who can dissemble, and who has the patience to wait for just the right moment. He is also the master of subtle, moderate and persuasive speech. When he leaves Calypso, he knows how to disarm her with flattering words:

> "My lady goddess, I beg you not to resent my feelings. I too know well enough that my wise Penelope's looks and stature are insignificant compared with yours. For she is mortal, while you have immortality and unfading youth." (5, 215,f)

And later, when he shows himself to Nausicaa "σμερδαλέος", a terrible sight, and "κεκαμωμένος ἅλμη", caked with salt, he knows how to flatter her as well:

> "Mistress, I throw myself on your mercy. But are you some goddess or a mortal woman ? If you are one of the gods who live in the sky, it is of Artemis, the Daughter of almighty Zeus, that your beauty, grace and stature most remind me. But if you are one of us mortals who live on earth, then lucky indeed are your father and gentle mother; lucky, your brothers too. How their hearts must glow with pleasure every time they see their darling join the dance!" (6, 149f).

By his ingenuity he defeats the cruel might of the Cyclopes (9, 303f); his prudence never deserts him, and his inventiveness is inexhaustible. He is one of those representative figures that mirror his whole race: Themistocles, Alcibiades, Theramenes, but also Juvenal's Graeculus , and even Michael Psellos and Eleftherios Venizelos are his descendants.

90

Nevertheless, as has been rightly pointed out, the fact that Athena follows his every step in the shape of a goddess or some mortal detracts from his greatness and lowers the suspense of the action. His exploits only really become exciting in his sea adventures, because then Athena is absent from his side. We know, it is true, that he will escape even without the assistance of the goddess; but still, when he has a divine protector by his side, interest in a hero is diminished.

Space does not permit us to enlarge on the other heroes of the epics, such as Ajax and Diomedes, or to write of all the noblewomen, like Penelope, Hecuba and Andromache. We must, however, add that Homeric narrative does not concentrate only on the great figures; it shows the same interest in minor and unimportant people, such as Axylus (VI, 13-15), Dresus (VI, 22), Meges (XV, 535f), Theano (VI, 298f) and Icmalius (19, 56-57); and it never scorns the humble person because he has no heroic elements in his character.

Thus epic poetry creates a completely human world. And while its myths and stock phrases link it with the past, it succeeds in integrating with the present and creating a harmonious whole, which embraces nearly every aspect of life. Its men and women - who are so alive because the epic carefully describes their inner world - constitute a splendid gallery of human types, together with all the characteristics which go to make up their personalities; and all without any criticism or comment on the poet's part. Greek learning held them up as examples, and for centuries the Greeks took the lives and exploits of these heroic models as their guide.

Before leaving the Homeric world of men, we should say a few words about the epic conception of the soul. The subject is obviously of great importance, not least because the Homeric epic has no word that corresponds exactly to what we mean by soul. The soul in Homer, (*psyche*), is closer to the sense of soul-breath, the spirit, or soul-shade, which leaves the body to spend a sorrowful existence in Hades. The soul of the living person is the seat of thought, of the emotions and desires. Basically, however, we know nothing of what they considered to be the nature of the soul at that time, or the way in which it was supposed to function (Snell 1955, 17; Harrison, 1960, 63).

As for human individuality, it is clear that in Homer human will and divine purpose are interwoven. The actions of men and the commands of the gods are two spheres that complement each other, but which may also clash. In this respect there is a difference between the Iliad and the Odyssey. In the later of the two epics as we have seen, it is emphasized that man makes his own decisions and takes entire responsibility for them. Later, in Attic tragedy, this problem, which has its roots in the Homeric epics (Lesky 1966, 71f), is presented in all its magnitude and with all its ramifications.

The world of the gods.

The world of the gods in Homer is a strange blend of naive superstition and subtle satire, which is certainly the outcome of a long-lived religious tradition. The older traditions of the Iliad obviously belong to the period when men looked on the Twelve Gods of Olympus with real awe. The later additions and modifications belong to the period when religious feeling in the Ionian world had changed - and perhaps much weakened.[9] In any case, the brilliantly contrived and often extraordinary scenes with the gods are an important element in epic art, and at the same time they assist the poet in organizing his vast and disparate material, because the scenes of the gods serve both as an explanation for and an aid to epic action.

Generally the gods live on Olympus,[10] whence they descend whenever they wish, to appear before mortals either in divine shape - always anthropomorphic[11]-or in the shape of a mortal.[12] The gods, like humans, have their rivalries and violent passions, and are sometimes even vulnerable, like Aphrodite in Iliad V, who was wounded by Diomedes.

Zeus alone is above all this. He never comes down to earth and never takes part in the battles of men or gods. He summons the assemblies of the gods, is the arbiter in their disputes and imposes his all-

9. In epic poetry the gods are morally inferior to humans; cf Schmid - Stählin 1929, 112.
10. In the Iliad, Olympus is generally a mountain in Thessaly (however cf I, 590f and VIII, 25, which may be late additions). In the Odyssey, Olympus is a palace in the sky (6, 42f) different from the mountain (11, 313. 315).
11. This is apparent from certain epithets used to characterize the gods, and which often anticipate the manner in which sculpture was later to portray them.
12. For example Athena in the Iliad (XXII, 226f) appears in the shape of Deiphobus, and in the Odyssey (2, 267f) in the shape of Mentor.

powerful will. Even the epithets used to characterize him are not those applicable to men ("ἀστεροπητής", god of lightening; "νεφεληγερέτα", the cloud-gatherer; "πατὴρ ἀνδρῶν τε θεῶν τε", father of men and of gods).

Behind the gods of Olympus, however, and over them, a dark, indeterminate force is at work, in the face of which Zeus himself is impotent: Moira. Hence in Iliad XXII the father of gods and men groans, when he is compelled to abandon Hector, the warrior who has offered him so many sacrifices on the peaks of Mount Ida, and then consults Moira (in the concrete form of a pair of scales) in order to learn what exactly is her will:

"....... The Father held out his golden scales, and putting sentence of death in either pan, on one side for Achilles, on the other for horse-taming Hector, he raised the balance by the middle of the beam. The beam came down on Hector's side, spelling his doom. He was a dead man. Phoebus Apollo deserted him ......" (XXII, 209-213)

The epic pantheon is composed of gods of different origins: besides father Zeus, the Indo-European sky god, we find Athena and Hera, palace-goddesses from the Mycenean age, and Asiatic deities like Ares, Aphrodite, Hephaestus, and probably Apollo. Also venerated as gods are winds, rivers, Eos, Erinyes and Eileithyia (Schmid - Stählin 1929 I, 1, 112). The rustic deities, however, are rarely mentioned, while personifications of abstract, moral concepts are completely absent from the Homeric epics, and there are no allusions to any involvements of the gods in natural events. The personifications found in the epics represent harmful daemoniacal powers, like *Phobos* (fear), *Deimos* (terror), *Eris* (discord), *Ossa* (rumour) or *Ate* (infatuation, folly, and its punishment, which are sent by the gods). But these personified concepts do not belong to the sphere of the gods.

The epic gives us the mythology not only of the heroes but of the gods as well, an aspect of the attitude towards the gods which basically is not a religious one. This divine mythology is about the relationships between the deities themselves, and especially about the way in which they are organized into a hierarchy, of which Zeus is the head.

This system - with Zeus as ruler of a community of gods - seems to belong to the Mycenean period, and to have some correspondence with its political organization; a powerful king like Agamemnon ruled over "all Argos and many islands" (cf II, 100; Nilsson 1933, 266f). Zeus, like Agamemnon, has inherited the kingship; the other gods are subordinate, and he summons them for consultation exactly as Agamemnon summons the other leaders of the Achaeans.

In the Homeric epics the hyperboles are never fantastic. In the world of men credibility is always maintained, which is why everything super-natural is attributed to the gods alone. For example, Aphrodite wraps Paris in a cloud as he is in the middle of a single-combat with Menelaus, and takes him back to Helen (III, 281f). Hera bestows on Xanthus, Achilles' immortal horse, a voice so that he can speak (XIX, 405). And in the Odyssey, it is Athena who changes Odysseus into a beggar (13, 397).

The supernatural element, which makes such an inept appearance in Virgil and is lifeless in most of the later epics, has a quality of spontaneous charm in Homer, a naivety which captivates the modern reader. Just as Achilles, in I, 194, feels no surprise at seeing Athena standing behind him at the moment when he is quarrelling with Agamemnon, equally the modern reader does not feel that the appearance of the goddess is something impossible or odd.

Originally the intervention of the gods was the consequence of man's impotence in the face of nature (cf Robert 1950, chap. 1); later, however, the rhapsodes exploited it in order to produce striking poetical effects, [13] or to give their plots a forward momentum. [14] In its extreme form, intervention by the gods took the form of the continuous escorting of a great hero by some deity, as Odysseus was continuously escorted and inspired by Athena in the Odyssey. [15]

---

13. The appearances of Thetis in the Iliad (XIX, 2f) and Athena in the Odyssey (20, 30f) belong to this category.
14. The transformation of Odysseus into a beggar by Athena belongs to this category.
15. The motif of the protection and guidance of a favoured mortal by a god had evolved long before the monumental Odyssey, as is clear from Athena's assistance of Tydeus in the Iliad, or Hera's protection of Jason (12, 72).

In contrast to humans, the Homeric gods are always happy. Only against this background of divine happiness is it possible to display clearly the ill-fortune and pain which are the lot of mortals. The happiness of the gods, of which we are witnesses right from the first book of the Iliad, is described with even greater power in XII and after. The long episode of the Beguilement of Zeus (Διὸς Ἀπάτης), which occupies the greater part of books XIII-XV, is perhaps the most typical example. It is a rich poetical creation, a few lines of which - those describing Poseidon driving his chariot across the sea - suffice to illustrate the total felicity of the gods, and how great the contrast with the incessant woes, cares, discord and death which prevail in the world of mortals :

"There he harnessed to his chariot his two swift horses, who had brazen hooves and flowing golden manes. He clothed himself in gold, picked up his well-made golden whip, mounted his chariot and drove out across the waves. The monsters of the sea did not fail to recognize their King. On every side they issued from their caves and gambolled at his coming. The sea itself made way for him in its delight, so that his bounding horses flew along, and the bronze axle of his chariot remained dry below as they carried him towards the Achaean fleet." (XIII, 25f).

How brightly all things to do with the gods sparkle, especially all their material possessions! It is true they resemble the objects used by the heroes, but they are incomparably more magnificent and precious.[16]

However, in the latest and most evolved stages of the Ionic epic, the gods are also represented as comic figures. The best known scene of this kind is in book I of the Iliad (599f), with its resounding Olympian laughter. It is a genuine comedy scene, because when Hephaestus is thrown out of Olympus, we know that he is not going to suffer any harm. And this divine comedy is continued and reaches a culmination in the Battle of the Gods in Iliad XX, in which all the gods, invulnerable as they are, smite each other heartily. This irreverence is never present in the relations between gods and humans, Nevertheless the real lyric sensitivity of many verses in some of the more comic parts of the epic show that the poet was composing comedy and not farce.

---

16. As examples, Hera's chariot (V, 722f) or the golden thrones of Hera and Athena (VIII, 436), etc. .

Thus the tragic plot of the Iliad unfolds against the backdrop of this Olympian comedy, and the more that human woes multiply and oppress the atmosphere, the more extravagant and comic the scenes of the gods become. It is, indeed, because of these scenes that the Iliad cannot be exclusively described as a 'great tragedy'. It is at the same time a comedy, and perhaps the only serious poetical work of the Western world that harmoniously interweaves tragic and comic emotions.

In contrast to the Iliad, the gods in the Odyssey play a much smaller role. They have a part, of course, in the development of the work, but with the exception of Athena,[17] their involvement in the plot is much looser. The idea of the gods' assemblies in Odyssey 1 and 5 - which are the only scenes of the gods in this epic - is clearly taken from the Iliad. But the noisy quarrelling of the Olympians in the Iliad is in complete contrast to the assembly in the Odyssey, which is full of tranquillity and godlike grandeur. In this epic Zeus, who always presides over the assemblies of the gods, does not impose his might by threats or force. Full of dignity, he personifies universal moral conscience, and begins his speech about Odysseus with a general reflection on the problem of human misfortune and the close relationship between men's destinies and their mistakes. In the Odyssey special stress is laid on the fact that the gods are not responsible for human misfortune (1, 32f), that they honour justice (14, 83), and that the evil are punished.[18] All through the Odyssey there is a clear attempt to justify the behaviour of the gods towards men. A religious and ethical ideal governs the myth which is woven about Odysseus' wanderings and the suitors' bad behaviour, which leads finally to their destruction.

Thus the Homeric epics operate on two planes, the divine and the human, and this gives the narrative a curious double aspect. Every event is looked at from two standpoints, according to whether it unfolds on earth or in the sky. The significance of this double aspect is that it reveals the limitations of all human action and the impotence of man, because in the final count he is dependant on the unfathomable decisions of powers which are over him and remote from him.

---

17. In the Iliad there is nothing comparable to the warm, continuous protection given to Odysseus by Athena.
18. Hence the new word "$\theta\epsilon o\upsilon\delta\acute{\eta}\varsigma$" (god-fearing).

Since the epic represents the gods as participating in all human affairs and misfortunes, it has simultaneously to examine the place of the gods in the world and their intrinsic eternal significance. It accomplished this by measuring all human actions according to moral and religious standards. Hence Greek epic poetry looked at life from a standpoint infinitely higher and more objective than did mediaeval epic poetry, and it gave a first shape to the anthropocentric conception that was later to prevail in ancient Greek civilization; one may justly say, as has often been said, that Homeric poetry contains the seeds of all Greek philosophy which developed subsequently.

In conclusion we should add that the Homeric conception of a world of gods, which is over the human one and which is constantly intervening in human affairs, had its influence on Virgil, Milton and Tasso, to mention only three great names, as well as on many of the epic parodies of more recent times.

CHAPTER SIX – THE POETIC ACHIEVEMENT OF THE HOMERIC EPICS.

The Homeric epics flout all the canons established by literary criticism as the hallmarks of great poetry. The language they employ is not a living idiom, but an artificial literary language that was never spoken in any part of the Greek world. The unit of expression is not the living word, but a series of ossified, conventionalized phrases, the formulas. Furthermore, the Homeric epics are not the works of one poet, but the creation to a great extent of many rhapsodes belonging to different periods.

As if this were not enough, the Homeric epics contain many composite descriptions of things and places which never existed in the form in which they are presented; they are full of contradictions, they interweave different versions of myths and episodes and their structure is purely 'episodic'. And yet the poetic achievement of the Iliad and Odyssey is superb. This is largely due to:

1) The simple dramatic manner in which the poet presents his material. Every figure - Agamemnon, Achilles, Odysseus, Hector, Paris - is always presented at some critical, dramatic moment, and the attitudes[1] of the heroes, while speaking and acting as adversaries, give the epics much of their liveliness and power. These scenes are never excessively protracted, and although some of them are certainly less gripping than others, they exhibit on the whole a wonderful economy of treatment. There are very few episodes in either epic which betray an "ornamental conception" of poetry or a weak linking of the parts constituting a dramatic unity.

In order to achieve the desired effect the encounters between the heroes must be encounters between men belonging to an ideal heroic world which excites our admiration and wonder.

This is why the people in the epic heroic world are portrayed as

_____

1. Attitude in the sense in which I. A. Richards (1959) uses the word.

idealized beings. The warriors are bigger, stronger and braver than 'contemporary men', the women are "white-armed", "fair-ankled", "well-girdled". The arms, chariots, houses, furniture, ornaments and implements are all magnificent. Gold, silver, ivory, and woollen and linen fabrics abound.

The close contact between the gods and the Homeric heroes (the gods, as we have seen, intervene for their own ends in the lives of humans, and many heroes are in fact descended from the gods) confers a special splendour on the world of mortals. And the epics never descend to low or unseemly descriptions.[2]

Thus the Homeric epics evoke in the hearer (or reader) the joy of a world which is 'ideal',[3] but in which nevertheless the supernatural and impossible do not have a place; because the improbable in a narrative always destroys the picture of the ideal. For this reason even when the Homeric epic exaggerates - and of course like every epic it does exaggerate - the exaggerations are never monstrous or gross; they stay within the limits of human possibility. For example Achilles is the strongest and fleetest of foot among the Achaeans, but never implausibly so. Agamemnon, Ajax and Odysseus may battle singlehanded against great odds, but there is nothing of the supernatural in their achievements, nothing approaching the exaggerations of the *Chanson de Roland,* in which Tourben kills four hundred of the enemy within the space of a few minutes! In the Homeric epics the supernatural is confined, as we have seen, to the world of the gods, where indeed it also belongs more acceptably.

Even in the Odyssey, in which a large part of the material derives from ancient tales and sea stories, the supernatural element is restrained and humanized; this is what makes it qualify as great poetry, in which credibility is always maintained; we have the feeling that we are in a world of reality and not of fairy tale. This impression is the more credible because no Homeric hero possesses magic powers. It has been

---

2. At the same time the 'mythical past', being static and not fluid like the present, offers examples which throw new light on the familiar aspects of life and lend them a deeper meaning.
3. Brilliant material very often inspires good poetry. In this respect Homer is like Virgil, Dante and Milton.

often and rightly stressed that one of the greatest achievements of Homeric poetry is its humanization of myth and legend.

Along with the pleasure afforded by this idealized element, the Homeric epics also project the tensity resulting from the tragic - heroic contradiction of life. This may be summed up as a despair which still may yield a harvest of glory. Perhaps the most perfect expression of this tragic - heroic concept is to be found in Sarpedon's words to Glaucus:

> "Ah, my friend, if after living through this war we could be sure of ageless immortality, I should neither take my place in the front line nor send you out to win honour in the field. But things are not like that. Death has a thousand pitfalls for our feet; and nobody can save himself and cheat him. So in we go, whether we yield the glory to some other man or win it for ourselves" (XII, 322-328)

We find the same spirit in Hector's famous reply to Andromache (VI, 441-465). There is an echo in these words, so simply and naturally expressed, of something transcending his own sadness - a father's and a husband's - , and transcending the sadness that hangs over all Troy. His is the voice of a man standing face to face with his destiny, at the very moment he is about to fulfil the great purpose of his life, the voice of a warrior who may be able to transform his poor human existence into a blaze of glory, by snatching victory from death.

This tragic attitude of epic poetry to life is heightened by the poetic artifice of casting the shadow of imminent catastrophe over every great triumph.

In Iliad XII, for example, when the Trojans are storming the wall of the Achaeans' camp, they see an omen which, according to the interpretation by Polydamas (195-250), is a warning to Hector that in the very moments of his triumph he is heading for his doom.[4] Or, to give another characteristic example, at the instant Achilles is about to kill Hector, the words of the vanquished hero cast the shadow of death over the victor's greatest triumph:

---

4.   Zeus has already said the same thing in XI, 207-209.

"Nevertheless pause before you act, in case the angry gods remember
how you treated me, when your turn comes and you are brought down
at the Scaean Gate in all your glory by Paris and Apollo."[5] (XXII, 358-360)

Thus the powerlessness of mortal men is underlined, while at the
same time the greatness of heroic achievement, which snatches glory
out of the midst of human weakness, is extolled.

If we turn now to the direct, simple narrative manner of the epic,
we can see that its lucidity is the result of the very acute observation of
the poet(or poets) and his (or their) natural analytical capabilities. The
most composite objects are separated into their characteristic components and, one by one, set out clearly before us. The Homeric epics shun
abstractions and generalities.

The poet sketches for us in a few lines a thing or a battle which a
prose-writer or historian would need many pages of detail to describe.
There is no superfluous detail in Homeric descriptions. What dominates
them is the dramatic or moral purpose which is their goal. Another
feature is the manner in which the epic portrays people, so as to give
simultaneously both their general 'type' traits and their individual
characteristics; Hector in the Iliad, for example, and Nausicaa in the
Odyssey are presented in this fashion.
2) The nobility and majesty given to the narrative by the hexameter
rhythm, and the richness, splendour and formality of the epic language.
In the Homeric epics unity of form and content is absolute; the form is
perfectly fitted to the material it encompasses and is no less brilliant.

The richness and splendour of epic expression are, naturally, due
not only to the vocabulary but also to the style - to the manner in
which the vocabulary is used. We have already touched on this subject;
here we must stress once more the significance of the three main components of epic style: the brilliant similes, which bring the narrative to
life (v. 60), the constant ornamental epithets, which confer nobility and
majesty on everything, and finally the restrained use of metaphor.
Because if any note of affectation is allowed to intrude into a majestic
style, the style immediately becomes false and grandiloquent; this

---

5.   The shadow of death lies over Achilles right from the start of the Iliad; cf I,
     416; XVIII, 95-96; XIX, 408. 416; XXI, 110; XXII, 358.

commonly results from an excessive use of metaphor.[6]

3)   Perhaps, however, the unique achievement of the Homeric epics is primarily due to the nobility and depth of the sentiments which are described. These range from a warrior's fierce thirst for honour to the tragic despair of a young wife saying farewell to her warrior husband; and from an old father's love for the dead body of his son to the delicate shyness of the young princess, and the joy of a man and his wife united again after many years of separation and misfortune.

The emotions described in the epic are usually depicted against the dark background of death, and this gives them a special power. Everything the person has loved and lost is depicted in the shadow of death, and this heroic nostalgia becomes an integral part of the epic atmosphere. Because the tragedy of each person's life is broadened to embrace the tragic destiny of all mankind.

Human sensitivity, however, is never allowed to descend to sentimentality. It is always portrayed bound up with the loftiest and manliest purposes, so that the harshness of war and memories of life are indissolubly joined. It must not be forgotten that behind the formality and nobility of Glaucus and Diomedes, and the civilized hospitality proffered at Pylos or on Scheria, there exists a harsh, primitive world. Hector is not always the devoted husband and father of Iliad VI, or the kindly brother-in-law of Helen. In XVII, 125 he drags away Patroclus' body to cut off the head and throw the body to the Trojan dogs, and in XVIII, 176f he proposes to impale Patroclus' head on a stake. And to mention one more example, Telemachus behaves almost brutally towards Penelope, and carries out his father's order to kill the guilty slave-women in the most cruel fashion (22, 443f. 462f).

These savageries, for all their horror, lend power and passion to the epic and, more importantly, are a reminder to us not to approach Homeric heroes with sentimentality.

6.   And v. Proclus' commentary on the *Timaeus* I. 20.

CHAPTER SEVEN — THE INFLUENCE OF THE HOMERIC EPICS.

The influence of the Homeric epics on Greek literature and civilization was vast; hence coming as they did, at the very beginning of Greek history, they may also in a sense be looked on as the educators of mankind. That this was so is due to their humanism and wide knowledge of life. And it must not be forgotten that for the ancient Greeks the poet was also a 'teacher' in the broadest sense.

Thus we see the later epic, elegiac and personal lyric poets lifting quotations straight out of Homer - the Cyclic Epics, Callinus, Tyrtaeus, Solon, Alcman, Alcaeus and Archilochus employed many words and phrases from the Homeric epics. Choral lyric poetry also drew on the Iliad and Odyssey, and the earlier epigrams and oracles made use of Homeric phrasal patterns.

The influence of the Homeric technique and language on Hesiod is marked, as it is on all didactic epic poetry. And yet Hesiod and, after him, the guilds of prophets and soothsayers of the 7th and 6th centuries were opposed to Homer in religious matters. Philosophers like Xenophanes and Heraclitus followed them in their hostility towards the Homeric gods, and similar condemnations continued right into the Christian era. At that time the dispute reached a new juncture in which the moral and aesthetic sides of Homeric study were clearly differentiated, because even the fiercest opponents of Homer did not dare to question his aesthetic value.

However not all the philosophers ranged themselves against Homer. The Pythagoreans, for example, cited his verses in support of their views, and allegorical interpretations of Homer made their appearance with Theagenes, Stesimbrotus, Glaucon and Anaxagoras.

In the 6th century BC when the city-state began to interest itself in the education of its citizens, the Homeric epics were included in the festival celebrations at Athens, for example, and Syracuse. This was why Plato was later able to say that Homer was the educator of the Greeks

(*Republic* 606 E), a view which had already been put forward in the form of an accusation by Xenophanes (Frag. 10 (11), Diehl). And indeed if we remember the enormous influence Homer had on Attic tragedy (Aeschylus called his own works 'crumbs' from the Homeric banquets) and the fact that History and Philosophical Discourse, the two forms of prose which exercised the greatest educational influence, were born of the clash between various philosophical opinions and epic poetry, then we are obliged to agree with Plato.

During the time of the sophists there was a particular interest in Homer, and this was also the time when Herodotus initiated the 'Homeric Question'.[1] Homer's influence spread not only to vase-painting (where it makes its appearance from the 7th century) but also to the works of the great 5th century artists, such as Pheidias, who was the leading figure of his time in sculpture and architecture, Polygnotus the great painter, and Polygnotus the vase-painter. At that time the Homeric conception of the Olympic gods was the one generally prevalent.[2]

Just how popular Homer was in the 5th century is apparent from the recitations of the rhapsodes, which were admired throughout the Greek world, as well as from the statue of Homer set up at Olympia at the beginning of the century. In the 4th century the recitations of the rhapsodes degenerated into bad theatrical appearances, as Plato tells us (*Ion,* and *Laws* II, 658 D). Further evidence of Homer's popularity is the fact that many of his verses became proverbial in antiquity.

In the 4th century, in spite of his admiration for Homer, Plato excluded his works from the Republic on moral grounds.[3] The Platonic

---

1. Herodotus, contrary to the general belief of his time that all the poems of the epic cycle were Homeric, maintained that the *Cypria* were not genuine. His opposition to the prevailing view was subsequently carried a stage further and culminated in Aristotle's statement that only the Iliad, the Odyssey and the comic poem *Margarites* were authentic works by Homer.
2. For Homer's influence on the figurative arts, v. Bethe 1922, 301f.
3. Plato maintained that Homeric poetry was an "imitation of an imitation", and consequently thrice removed from the truth and for this reason misleading; furthermore, it gave a false picture of the gods and a terrifying picture of death. He was also of the opinion that Homer's poetry was directed at the two lower parts of the soul - emotion and desire - and prevented the functioning of the upper part - reason - which restrains and controls the two lower ones.

view was followed by the cynic Zoilus in his bitter attack on Homer. Aristotle was of the opposite opinion; his approval and admiration of Homer were boundless, and he passed on his admiration to his pupil, Alexander. Alexander's successors followed in his footsteps and under their patronage the Homeric studies of the Alexandrian scholars flourished.

The work of the Alexandrian scholars, chiefly Zenodotus, Aristophanes of Byzantium, and Aristarchus laid the basis on which every serious study of the Homeric epics has been founded. The Alexandrians studied Homer from every angle - linguistic, metrical, mythological, aesthetic etc. . Their studies were supplemented by the historian-archaeologists of Pergamum, Crates of Mallos, Demetrius of Scepsis and Polemon of Ilium. After them all real work on the Homeric epics came to a halt, although the sterile debate over Plato's condemnation of poetry and the Pergamenes' allegorical interpretation of the Homeric gods continued until the end of the ancient world.

Above all, however, Homer became the basic school book of the Hellenistic world; this is clear from the large number of papyri that have been found. As a school book it had indeed been in use since the 6th century,[4] although in that period only fragments of the poems were taught, mainly by the rhapsodes, and preference was given to the Iliad, particularly the first books.[5]

Besides the scholars and teachers, the Hellenistic poets - who often combined the functions of poet and scholar - also continually drew on Homer, especially when writing in the dactylic hexameter. Callimachus, for instance, in his refined, carefully worked verse, refers indirectly to Homer, and Apollonius Rhodius in his great epic, the *Argonauts,* makes more direct reference to him while still avoiding the juxtaposition of straight Homeric lines or parts of lines.

4.　　v. Schmid - Stählin 1927 I, 1, 174. Numbers of Greeks in the 6th, 5th and 4th centuries knew all of the Homeric epics by heart. cf Kirk, 1966, 173.
5.　　The diffusion and importance of the Homeric epics in post-Classical antiquity is apparent both from the exercises in rhetoric and from different popular philosophical treatises which drew on Homer for their themes.

One need not refer here to the didactic epic of Hellenistic times, but we should mention the fact that, as we travel further away from the Classical period, the former ancient inspiration, which was gradually dying out, turned once more to Homer, the great model of Greek genius. Nevertheless Quintus Smyrnaeus in his '*Posthomerica*' is nothing but a lifeless imitator, and Nonnus, who represents the last glimmer of the great epic in the 5th century AD, is longwinded and full of Eastern bombast.

The aesthetic brilliance of the Homeriç poems was such as to cause the Greeks of Christian Byzantium to reject finally their moral and religious content (along with the moral and religious precepts of all Greek poetry) in order to enjoy their aesthetic perfection. Hence we arrive on the one hand at the 'Homerocentrones', that is the poetic patchworks of Homeric lines and half-lines - like those produced by the Empress Eudocia and the Philosopher Optimus - and, on the other hand, at the great Byzantine church sages, like Photius and Eustathius, who were at the same time prelates of the Church and great admirers and students of Homer.

Turning to the West and Homer's influence there, we meet with a whole string of famous names. Foremost among them undoubtedly is Virgil, whose *Aeneid* occupied a unique position in Western culture. In the last centuries of the ancient world, throughout the Middle Ages and Renaissance, and almost up to the French Revolution, Virgil and not Homer was the greatest epic poet in Western eyes. Nor must we forget the other Roman poets of the Augustan era who were influenced by Homer, or the fundamental importance for the development of Roman poetry of the Latin translation of the Odyssey by Livius Andronicus (3rd century BC), or the influence of Homer on Ennius.

A long series of epic poets followed in Virgil's wake, from Valerius Flaccus to Claudian, and from Claudian to Ariosto. All of them were greatly indebted to the Homeric epics, even if the debt is often an in-direct one. Dante's *Divine Comedy* has of course a special place in Mediaeval literature, and there is no need to repeat how much its author owed to Virgil and therefore indirectly to Homer.

In the 15th century, when the Renaissance was bearing its first fruits, there was a revival of admiration for Homer (Finsler 1912), although we have no direct imitators of him in the Italian literature of the period.[6] In the 16th century the French Pléiade, headed by Pierre Ronsard, roughly contemporary with Ariosto, displayed a special enthusiasm for Homer, and from then on the 'blind minstrel's' fame started to rival that of Virgil. The reaction to the Pléiade movement - led by François Malherbe - was conspicuous among the greatest French writers of the 17th century, when 'common sense', 'good taste' and 'naturalism' were the literary watchwords, but then these virtues, together with 'majesty', were also discovered in Homer by Louis XIV's generation.

Mention should also be made of Milton's attempt to compose in contemporary idiom an epic similar in style and form to the Homeric epics, as well as the influence exercised on English thought and 18th century poetry by Alexander Pope's translation of the Iliad.[7]

When the theories of Wolf and particularly Lachmann, who regarded Homeric poetry, at least in origin, as folk verse, received recognition, the critics almost unanimously gave first place to Homer over Virgil, because the *Aeneid* appeared artificial in comparison with the Homeric epics. This trend in scholarly criticism was further reinforced by the work of Johann Joachim Winckelmann[8] and his definition of Classical art as "noble simplicity and quiet greatness" ("eine edle Einfalt und eine stille Grösse"). This was the conception which inspired Lessing in his *Laokoon*; it was adopted with enthusiasm and remained predominant until the age of Romanticism. Thus during the transition from the 18th to the 19th century the Homeric epics were considered to be an expression of 'absolute beauty', outside the bounds of time and place.

6. The first edition of Homer (*editio princeps*) was published, as we have seen, in 1488 by Demetrius Chalcondyles.
7. It should be noted that the interest of the English in Homer began with the translations of G. Chapman and A. Pope, and that the first treatise by R. Wood, *An Essay on the Original Genius and Writings of Homer,* which was published in Dublin in 1769, opened the way to the study and appreciation of Homer's work by the Germans; because it was the views of the English scholars that influenced Lessing, Herder, Goethe and Heine.
8. It is well known that Wincklemann, comparing Classical and Baroque art, declared the former to be far superior.

The leaders and groups of the Romantic movement, however, although admiring Homer, were not influenced directly by him because they regarded the Iliad and Odyssey as 'impersonal' works, which did not accord with their conception of art as a form of subjective, personal expression.

Finally Matthew Arnold's contribution to the understanding of Homer's art in the Anglo-Saxon world should be singled out, and the fact emphasized that from the 19th century to the present day Homer has received worldwide recognition as the founder and unchallenged king of the Classical tradition.

We shall conclude with the observation, apropos the history of Hellenism, that the teaching of Homer in Greek schools has continued without interruption from the 6th century BC to our own time. Naturally the Homeric epics were taught in different fashions at different periods and in different Greek schools. It is nevertheless a fact that not a single educated generation of Greeks has grown up without having received some sort of instruction in Homer, and this surely constitutes the longest and perhaps most illustrious educational tradition in all the Western world.

INDEX

Abas 18

Achaeans 7-9, 11-15, 18, 22-24, 64, 72, 76, 81, 85, 94, 95, 100.

Achilles 3, 4, 7-9, 11-25, 29, 31, 40, 41, 50, 52, 59, 61, 64, 68, 69, 70-72, 91-89, 93, 94, 98-101.

Acousilaus 1.

Aeneas 18, 21, 60, 61, 69, 70.

Aeneid 21, 35, 77, 106, 107.

Aeolus 32.

Aeschines 25.

Aeschylus 16, 104.

Aethiopis 25.

Agamemnon 7, 9, 11, 13, 14, 20, 51, 53, 68, 71, 81, 85, 87, 94, 98, 99.

Aias 69, 72, and v. Ajax.

Ajax 9, 13, 14, 20, 23, 24, 68, 69, 86, 91, 99.

Alcaeus 103.

Alcibiades 90.

Alcinous 32, 52, 73, 80, 83.

Alcman 2, 54, 103.

Alexander 105.

Alexandrian 1, 10, 37, 57, 58, 75, 105.

Allen, T. W. 1, 5, 56.

Amphidamas 15.

Analysts 3, 5, 29, 33, 37.

Anaxagoras 103.

Andromache 12, 23, 24, 52, 82, 91, 100.

Aphrodite 23, 51, 92-94.

Apollo 2, 7, 60, 64, 77, 93, 101.

Apollo, *Hymn to* 2.

Apollodorus 48.

Apollonius Rhodius 6, 73, 105.

Archilochus 54, 103.

Ares 23, 93.

Arete 80.

arete 13, 81, 84, 85, 89.

Argonauts 35, 105.

Argos 1, 57, 94.

Argos 32, 39.

Ariosto 106, 107.

Aristarchus 24, 35, 37, 48, 56-58, 105.

aristeia 11, 12, 20-22, 25, 68.

Aristophanes of Byzantium 37, 57, 105.

Aristotle 8, 42, 75, 76, 85, 104, 105.

Arnold, M. 108.

Artemis 90.

Asclepius 2.

Asiatic 80, 93.

Asteris 39.

Athena 22, 32, 33, 45, 47, 53, 91-96.

Athenians 56.

Athens 1, 42, 56, 57, 103.

d'Aubignac, F. H. 3.

Augustan 106.

Axylus 91.

Bassett, S. E. 59, 62.

Bathycles 71.

Batrachomyomachia 2.

Bechtel, F. 42.

Bergk, T. 1, 2, 4.

Bethe, E. 4, 14, 24, 35, 56, 104.

Blass, F. 61.

Bowra, C. M. 5, 9, 30, 42.

Briseis 7.

Bucholtz, E. 65.

Bury, J. B. 4, 14, 29.

Busolt, G. 15.

Byzantines 75.

Byzantium 106.

Callimachus 105.

Callinus 2, 54, 103.

Calypso 32, 52, 73, 90.

Carpenter, R. 38, 56.
Caskey, J. L. 53.
Cauer, P. 4, 24, 35, 56, 74.
Caystrus 30.
Chadwick, H. M. 6, 43.
Chadwick, N. K. 6.
Chalcocondyles, D. 57, 107.
Chalcon 71.
Chanson de Roland 99.
Chantraine, P. 4, 42-45.
Chapman, G. 107.
Charis 51.
Charybdis 32.
Chios 1, 27, 29, 57.
Chorizontes 1.
Christ, W. 4.
Chromius 9.
Chrysa 7.
Chryseis 7.
Chryses 7, 18, 19, 64.
Cicero 25, 56.
Ciconians 32.
Cimmerians 32.
Circe 32, 37, 51.
Claudian 106.
Colophon 1, 29.
Cook, J. M. 54.
Crates of Mallos 105.
Cretan 81.
Crete 53, 57.
Croiset, M. 61.
Cyclopes 32, 34, 39, 72, 90.
Cynaethus 1.
Cypria 2, 104.
Cyprus 57,
Daedalus 72.
Dante 35, 99, 106.
Dares 18.
Davison, J. A. 1, 2, 56.
Deiphobus 22, 92.
Delebécque, E. 66, 67.
Delian festival 25.
Delos 25.

Demetrius of Scepsis 105.
Demodocus 2, 41.
Demosthenes 2.
Desborough, V. R. d'A. 47.
Diehl, E. 104.
Diels, H. 2.
Digenes Akritas 70.
Diogenes Laertius 26, 56.
Diomedes 11, 20, 21, 23, 51, 60, 68, 77, 80, 91, 92, 102.
Dioscuri 51.
Dodds, E. R. 3, 23.
Doerpfeld, W. 39.
Dorians 47.
Drerup, E. 4.
Dresus 91.
Duckworth, G. E. 64.
Düntzer, H. 44.

Eileithyia, 93.
Elpenor 37.
Ennius 106.
Eos 93.
Epeigeus 15.
Eratosthenes 39.
Erinyes 93.
Euboea 1.
Eudocia 106.
Eumaeus 32, 60.
Eurycleia 50.
Eurydamas 18, 52.
Eustathius 106.
Fenik, B. 10, 25, 66.
Fick, A. 42.
Finley, M. J. 25, 50, 80.
Finsler, G. 3, 74, 107.
Flaccus, V. 106.
Florence, 57.
Focke, F. 4, 35.
Fraccaroli, G. 64,
Fränkel, H. 74.
Friedländer, P. 2.

Geffcken, J. 38.
Geometric 8, 22, 28, 29, 48, 54.
Girard, P. 12.
Glaucon 103.
Glaucus 11, 16, 21, 80, 100, 102.
Glotz, G. 14.
Goethe 107.
Gray, D. H. F. 47, 53, 54, 66.
Grote, G. 3.
Hades 34, 35, 38, 52, 86, 91.
Hampe, R. 47
Hampl, F. 25.
Harrison, E. 91.
Hector 7-9, 12, 19-25, 31, 48, 50-52, 59,
    68, 69, 81-84, 87, 89, 93, 98, 100-102.
Hecuba 80, 91.
Heine, H. 107.
Helen 7, 9, 22, 23, 81, 89, 94, 102.
Hentze, K. 62.
Hephaestus 24, 25, 51, 72, 75, 93, 95.
Hera 93-95.
Heracles 71.
Heraclitus 2, 103.
Herder, J. G. 3, 107.
Hermann, G. 3.
Hermes 18, 19, 32, 51.
Herodotus 56, 78, 104.
Hesiod 11, 54, 103.
Heubeck, A. 24.
Hipparchus 56.
Hittite 41.
Homeric Question 3, 5, 104.
Homeric Hymns 54.
Homeridae 1, 27.
Howald, E. 5.
Icarian Sea 30.
Icmalius 91.
Ida 93.
Idaeus 18.
Idomeneus 23, 69, 70.
Ionia 29, 39, 56.
Ios 1.
Iphidamas 71.

Iris 51, 77.
Irus 44.
Ischia 54.
Ithaca 1, 32-34, 39, 53, 80, 90.
Jacoby, F. 2, 48, 50, 53.
Jaeger, D. L. 11, 68.
Jason 94.
Jebb, R. 3, 4, 29.
Jones, W. 13.
Juvenal 90.
Kakrides, I. T. 5, 25.
Kirchoff, A. 4, 33.
Kirk, G. S. 2, 8, 12, 19, 28, 34, 37, 38,
    43, 53-55, 105.
Kohl, J.W. 1.
Kritheis 1.
Lachmann, K. 3, 107.
Laertes 18, 37.
Lang, A. 4.
Laothoe 80.
Latte, K. 14, 16.
Leaf, W. 4, 12, 19, 29.
Lefkas 39.
Lesky, A. 3, 21, 25, 66, 75, 92.
Lessing, G. E. 107.
Leucothee 60.
Leumann, M. 45.
Lipsius, J. H. 14.
Livius Andronicus 106.
Lorimer, L. H. 5, 66.
Lotus-eaters 32.
Louis XIV 107.
Lycaon 18.
Lycian 11.
Lycophron 15.
Lycurgus 26, 56.
Malherbe, F. 107.
Marathon 15.
Margarites 2, 104.
Marseilles 57.
Mazon, P. 4, 10, 17, 26, 27, 56, 57.
Medon 15.
Megarians 56.

Meges 91.
Meillet, A. 5.
Meistor, K. 43, 75.
Melanippus 60.
Meleager 25.
Meles 1.
Melesigenes 1.
Memnon 25.
Menelaus 7, 9, 20, 22, 23, 52, 60, 68, 70, 94.
Mentor 92.
Merkelbach, R. 4.
Meuli, K. 35.
Meyer, E. 4.
Milton 97, 99, 107.
Minos 35.
Minoan 41.
Moira 93.
Monro, D. B. 19, 49, 64.
Muehll, P. 4.
Murray, G. 4, 12, 25.
Muses 60.
Mycale 25.
Mycenae 29, 47, 89.
Mycenean 25, 30, 41, 42, 46, 47, 50, 66, 67, 79, 81, 89, 93, 94.
Mylonas, G. E. 29.
Myres, J. H. 8.
Myrmidons 7, 16.
Nausicaa 32, 39, 52, 80, 83, 84, 90, 101.
Necromancy 35.
Neleus 18.
Nestor 9, 11, 18, 20, 32, 47, 48, 54, 71, 76.
Nilsson, M. P. 11, 47, 94.
Niobe 30.
Nitsch, G. W. 68.
Nonnus 106.
Oceanus 72.
Odysseus 9, 13, 23, 32-40, 48, 50-53, 68, 70-72, 77, 78, 80, 83, 84, 86, 90, 94, 96, 98, 99.
Ogygia 32, 35.

Olympia 86, 104.
Olympians 34, 96.
Olympus 32, 86, 92, 93, 95.
Onomacritus 56.
Optimus 106.
Orestes 16.
Orion 35.
Orpheus 1, 56.
Page, D. L. 2, 4, 9, 10, 15, 24, 25, 30, 33-37, 48, 49, 53, 67, 77.
Palamas, K. 72.
Palmer, L. R. 11, 42, 57.
Panathenaea 3, 26, 27, 56.
Pandarus 11, 18, 23.
Panionian festival 25.
Paris 7, 9, 20, 22, 23, 68, 69, 94, 98, 101.
Parry, A. 5, 30.
Parry, M. 5, 6, 44, 75.
Patroclus 7, 11-17, 20-23, 31, 59, 60, 64, 67, 69, 70, 87, 89, 102.
Pausanias 2, 56.
Peisander, 20.
Peisistratus 3, 11, 27, 30, 56.
Peleus 15, 17, 41, 72, 86, 87.
Penelope 32, 33, 36, 37, 52, 80, 90, 91, 102.
Pergamum 105.
Pestalozzi, H. 5.
Pfeiffer, R. 1, 57.
Phaeacians 32, 34, 35, 38, 71, 80, or
Phaenops, 18.
Phegeus 18.
Pheidias 86, 104.
Phemius 41.
Philoetius 32.
Phoenicia 53.
Phoenicians 47, 53.
Phoenix 9, 13, 15, 86.
Phorcys 73.
Photius 106.
Phthia 15, 81.
Pindar 1.
Plataea 15.

Platnauer 42, 43.
Plato 10, 60, 103-105.
Pléiade 107.
Polemon of Ilium 105.
Polyctor 18.
Polydamas 100.
Polygnotus 104.
Polyidus 18.
Pope, A. 107.
Porzig, 43.
Poseidon 61, 95.
Priam 7, 8, 18, 19, 23, 71, 80, 82, 83, 87, 88.
Proclus 102.
Protesilaos 9.
Psellos, M. 90.
Pseudo-Longinus 49.
Pseudo-Plato 26, 56.
Pylades 16.
Pylaemenes 9.
Pylos 1, 11, 32, 102.
Pythagorians 103.
Quintilian 61.
Quintus Smyrnaeus 20, 106.
Reichel, W. 65.
Reinhardt, K. 5, 50.
Richards, I.A. 98.
Ridgeway, W. 29.
Risch 43.
Robert, C. 4.
Robert, F. 94.
Rohde, E. 35.
Ronsard, P. 107.
Roman 106.
Rothe, C. 4.
Ruijgh, C. J. 42.
Saint-Beuve 61.
St. George 70.
Sarpedon 11, 16, 20, 22, 59, 64, 100.
Schadewaldt, W. 5, 25.
Schedius 9.
Scheria 32, 35, 39, 52, 73, 102.
Schmid, W. 1-3, 16, 19, 88, 92, 93, 105.

Schultze, W. 42.
Schwyzer, E. 42.
Scott, L. A. 4.
Scylla 32.
Semonides of Amorgos 2.
Sheppard, J. T. 4, 19.
Shipp, G. T. 74.
Sicyon 2.
Sipylus 30.
Sirens 32.
Sirius 69, 74.
Sisyphus 35, 76.
Smyrna 1.
Snell, B. 91.
Snodgrass, A. 47. 53.
Solon 56, 103.
Sparta 32, 34, 52.
Stählin, O. v. Schmid.
Stesimbrotus 103.
Strabo 1.
Stubbings, F. H. 1, 42.
Syracuse 103.
Talthybius 2.
Tantalus 35.
Tasso, 97.
Teiresias 51.
Telemachus 32-34, 36, 51, 77, 78, 102.
Theagenes 103.
Theano 91.
Thebais 2, 77.
Theiler, W. 4.
Themistocles 90.
Theoclymenus 36, 64.
Theocritus 73.
Theopompus 2.
Theramenes 90.
Thermopylae 15.
Thersites 9, 23, 68, 79.
Thessaly 92.
Thetis 13, 17, 45, 72, 86, 87, 94.
Thiaki 39.
Thoon 18.
Thrace 29.

113

Thrinacie 32.
Thucydides 2, 10.
Tityus 35.
Tourben 99.
Trojans 7, 22-24, 31, 70, 73, 80-82, 89, 100.
Troy 7, 8, 12, 22-25, 32, 51, 67, 69, 77 82, 89, 90, 100.
Trypanis, K. A. 14, 66, 68.
Turnus 21.
Tyrtaeus 2, 54, 103.
Unitarians 3-5, 29.
Venizelos, E. 90.
Virgil 21, 35, 77, 94, 97, 99, 106, 107.
Wace, A. J. B. 42.
Wackernagel, J. 42, 56.
Wade-Gery, H. T. 5, 26.
Webster, T. B.L. 8, 24.

von Wilamowitz-Moellendorff, U. 4, 12, 24, 28, 29, 31, 42, 88.
Winckelmann, J. J. 107.
Witte, K. 42, 43.
Wolf, F. A. 3, 6, 107.
Wolf, H. J. 13.
Wolf-Hartmut, F. 67.
Wood, R. 3, 6, 107.
Woodhouse, W. J. 5.
Xanthus 18.
Xanthus, Achilles horse 94.
Xanthus, river 75.
Xenophanes 2, 103, 104.
Xenophon 48.
Zenodotus 10, 56, 57, 105.
Zeus 8-11, 13, 45, 46, 50, 63, 71, 77, 83, 86, 90, 92-96, 100.
Zoilus 105.